Classic
CHICKEN DISHES

Classic
CHICKEN DISHES

Sue Ashworth • Jennie Berresford • Judy Bowen • Judy Bugg
Carole Handslip • Jane Hartshorn • Kathryn Hawkins
Cara Hobday • Deh-ta Hsiung • Louise Steele
Rosemary Wadey • Pamela Westland

P
•PARRAGON•

First published in Great Britain in 1997 by
Parragon
Unit 13–17
Avonbridge Trading Estate
Atlantic Road
Avonmouth
Bristol BS11 9QD

ISBN:
0-7525-2158-6 (hdbk)
0-7525-2210-8 (ppbk)

Printed in Italy

Edited, designed and produced by Haldane Mason, London

Acknowledgements
Editor: Christine McFadden
Design: Digital Artworks Partnership Ltd
Photography: Karl Adamson, Sue Atkinson, Iain Bagwell, Martin Brigdale,
Amanda Heywood, Joff Lee, Patrick McLeavey and Clive Streeter
Home Economists: Sue Ashworth, Jennie Berresford, Joanna Craig, Jill Eggleton,
Nicola Fowler, Carole Handslip, Jane Hartshorn, Kathryn Hawkins, Cara Hobday,
Deh-ta Hsiung, Wendy Lee, Louise Steele, Rosemary Wadey, Pamela Westland
Additional Recipes: Cara Hobday
Additional Photography: Iain Bagwell

Material in this book has previously appeared in *Balti Cooking, Barbecues,
Cajun & Creole Cooking, Caribbean Cooking, Chinese Cantonese Cooking,
Chinese Szechuan Cooking, Classic Home Cooking, Classic Indian Cooking,
The Complete Book of Italian Cooking, Cooking For One & Two,
Cooking On A Budget, Hot & Cold Sandwiches, Italian Regional Cooking,
Low-Fat Cooking, Mexican Cooking, Pasta Dishes, Picnics,
Quick & Easy Indian Cooking, Quick & Easy Meals,
Recipes with Yogurt, Sensational Salads, Soups & Broths, Thai Cooking,
Thai Side Dishes* and *Wok Cooking*.

Note
Cup measurements in this book are for American cups.
Tablespoons are assumed to be 15 ml. Unless otherwise stated, milk is assumed to be
full-fat, eggs are standard size 3 and pepper is freshly ground black pepper.

CONTENTS

INTRODUCTION

The 19th century French gastronome Brillat-Savarin was right when he wrote that 'Poultry is for the cook what canvas is to the painter.' When it comes to cooking chicken, the options are endless. Depending on the size of the bird and the cut, chicken can be stir-fried, sautéd, grilled (broiled), baked, roasted or casseroled. However you choose to cook it, there's no doubt that chicken gets top marks for versatility.

It's hardly surprising, therefore, that chicken has an established presence in every national cuisine. Descended from a Malaysian jungle fowl known as a mound bird, chickens were first domesticated in the Indus valley as long ago as 2500 BC, although they did not find their way to the Western world until much later. The Romans are said to have incubated huge quantities of eggs kept warm with the steam from hot underground springs – their knowledge of central heating must certainly have helped with this. We have the Romans to thank for the invention of the capon – a large male bird with succulent, tasty flesh. They circumvented a law forbidding the consumption of fattened chickens, which were a much-loved delicacy, by castrating cockerels. These emasculated birds grew to twice their normal size but without any loss of flavour.

Ease of rearing and the eggs produced must have contributed to the chicken's universal popularity, but there's little doubt that its value lay in the amazing variety of dishes to which it was suited. The French *poule au pot* is a homely chicken and vegetable casserole, fragrant with herbs and wine. Tandoori chicken, an Indian speciality, is made with skinless jointed chicken marinated in yogurt and spices before roasting in the fierce heat of the tandoor oven. The Italians like to sauté chicken joints with tomatoes and garlic, or grill (broil) whole baby chickens spatchcock-style over a rosemary-scented wood fire. In the Middle East, a whole chicken is slowly simmered with nuts or dried fruit. In South-East Asia small boneless chunks of chicken are stir-fried with fragrant aromatics such as ginger, chillies, lemon grass and garlic.

Tasty, nutritious, and easy on the pocket and waistline, chicken is the perfect choice for family meals, special occasion dinners, parties, barbecues and picnics. It's packed with protein and B vitamins, and, if you trim off the skin, it contains very little fat – 125 g/4 oz of lean flesh contains only 108 calories.

On the following pages you'll discover for yourself a marvellous selection of classic chicken dishes to add to your repertoire. The recipes include old favourites, such as Traditional Roast Chicken, Coq au Vin and Chicken Kiev, as well as less familiar but nevertheless classic creations from around the world. Try Baton Rouge Chicken Gumbo from America's Deep South, or Bang-Bang Chicken from China, or Chicken with 40 Garlic Cloves from France. Whatever your level of skill, the easy-to-follow step-by-step instructions will guarantee you success every time.

BUYING GUIDE

*When buying fresh chicken, check that it is well-chilled
and still within its sell-by date. Make sure that frozen chicken is still
frozen solid. A fresh chicken should have a soft, evenly coloured skin that feels
smooth and almost powdery-dry to touch. It should smell clean and fresh with no 'off'
taints. With prepacked chicken the clingfilm (plastic wrap) smoothes out signs of age, so it's harder
to evaluate the freshness. However, the flesh should feel plump and give slightly when
pressed, and young birds should have a pliable breastbone.*

Baby chicken The terms baby chicken, poussin, Cornish game hen and squab have different meanings in different countries, but in general they all refer to a 6-week-old, 500 g–1 kg/1–2 lb bird, which is small enough to serve whole to one person.

Boiling fowl These are large birds over 10 months old, with a good flavour, ideal for the casserole or for making stock. They are too tough for roasting or grilling (broiling).

Bresse chicken Reared in Bresse in the Burgundy region of France, these birds are rated as having the most superior flavour by countless chefs all over the world. They are reared in free-range conditions on high quality natural feed. They are expensive and available only from specialist shops.

Broiler or frying chicken These birds are reared to produce tender flesh, and are usually 6–8 weeks old, weighing 1.5–2 kg/3–4 lb. They are best used jointed and grilled (broiled) or fried, but whole birds can also be roasted, steamed or casseroled.

Capon These are large, castrated cockerels, about 10 weeks old, weighing as much as 5 kg/10 lb. They have a greater proportion of white meat and the flesh is

delicately marbled with fat which gives it an excellent flavour. A capon makes a good alternative to turkey for a special occasion.

Corn- or maize-fed chicken These are reared on a diet containing large amounts of sweetcorn – a feeding method popular in south-west France. The corn or maize is thought to give the bird a better flavour. However, flavour depends on other factors too, such as type of breed and whether or not the bird has been reared free-range, so a yellow-fleshed chicken may not necessarily taste better than a white one.

Free-range chicken Free-range chickens have the freedom to feed at will and space to run free, either in large airy barns or the farmyard. Barn-reared birds are slaughtered at 8–10 weeks, and farmyard birds at 10–12 weeks. They have a bigger, broader shape than the factory-reared broiler or roaster, and usually a better flavour.

Roaster These weigh about 1.8–3.5 kg/4–8 lb and are about 10 weeks old when slaughtered. Best roasted whole, but if they are not too large, they can be jointed and used for frying or grilling (broiling).

Spring chicken Also known as a double poussin, this is a 9- to 12-week-old bird, weighing about 1.25 kg/2½ lb, large enough to feed two.

FOOD SAFETY

Chicken is particularly prone to contamination by salmonella bacteria which can cause serious food poisoning.

- After buying, take your chicken home quickly, preferably in a freezer bag or cool box.

- Return frozen birds immediately to the freezer.

- Remove the wrapping from a chilled bird and place in a shallow dish to catch any drips.

- Cover loosely with foil and store on the bottom shelf of the fridge for no more than two or three days, depending on the sell-by date.

- Frozen birds should be thoroughly defrosted before using. If time permits, defrost for about 36 hours in the fridge; otherwise for about 12 hours in a cool room.

- Equipment, hands and sink must always be washed very thoroughly after handling raw flesh.

In any recipe, chicken must always be cooked all the way through. Never partially cook chicken with the intention of completing cooking later on. Bacteria can multiply at an alarming rate in a very short space of time. Test for doneness by inserting a skewer into the thickest part of the thigh – the juices should run clear without the slightest hint of pink.

COOKING CHICKEN

Chicken is one of the most versatile foods and can be cooked in a variety of ways.

Sautéing and pan-frying
Small thighs, drumsticks and joints can be fried in about 3 cm/1½ inches of groundnut oil in a large frying pan (skillet). Heat the oil to 180°C/350°F, or test by putting a cube of bread into the hot oil. If it browns in 1 minute, the oil is hot enough. Fry the chicken pieces all over, with or without a coating of seasoned flour, until they are an even golden brown. Then reduce the heat and fry for another 20–30 minutes until cooked through. The exact cooking time depends on size and thickness. Drain well on crumpled paper towel before serving.

Stir-frying
The key to successful stir-frying is to cut boneless meat into similar-sized pieces – either strips, small cubes or thin slices. That way, the meat cooks evenly and remains juicy. Preheat the wok or pan before adding a small amount of groundnut oil. When the oil starts to smoke add the chicken pieces and stir-fry with your chosen flavourings for 3–4 minutes until cooked through. Other ingredients can be cooked at the same time, or the chicken can be cooked by itself, then removed from the pan while you stir-fry the remaining ingredients. Return the chicken to the pan briefly when the other ingredients are cooked.

Grilling (broiling)
Grilling (broiling) is a sure-fire method of bringing out the best in chicken. The intense heat of the grill (broiler) quickly seals the juicy, succulent flesh beneath a golden, crispy exterior. Although the technique appears simple, success depends on speed, timing, correct distance from the heat source, and good quality ingredients. For instance, if you grill (broil) at too high a temperature and too close to the heat source, the outside of your chicken will be burnt before the inside is cooked. Too little heat for too long will dry it out. The chicken should be placed 10–15 cm/4–6 inches away from a moderate heat source. Young birds, such as a baby chicken (poussin), spring chicken or small roaster, are the most suitable candidates for grilling (broiling) as these are least likely to dry out and become too tough.

In order to brown evenly, the meat should be reasonably flat and compact. Even a small whole chicken needs to be cut into joints, or split down the backbone and flattened – a technique known as spatchcocking. The heat can then penetrate evenly. Chicken quarters are best reduced to smaller cuts. Divide leg portions into thighs and drumsticks. Breast meat, which can be slightly dry and dense, is best divided into bite-sized chunks for kebabs, or sliced and pounded flat to make escalopes. Wings are perfect for speedy grilling (broiling) – the bones disperse the heat and the skin traps moisture – making a delightful and very succulent dish.

Roasting

With crisp, golden-brown skin and moist succulent meat, a perfectly roasted chicken is an all-time delight. The best chickens for roasting usually weigh 1.8–2.7 kg/4–6 lb. When you're ready to cook, remove any lumps of fat from the opening to the body cavity. Rinse the bird inside and out under cold running water, then pat dry with paper towels. Season the cavity generously with salt and freshly ground black pepper, and insert stuffing or herbs as desired.

Place the bird on a rack in a roasting tin, then brush the skin all over with oil or melted butter, or rub with softened butter. Baste the bird two or three times with the pan juices during roasting. Alternatively, if you cover the chicken with a piece of muslin dipped in melted butter, you won't need to baste at all. Always check that the chicken is thoroughly cooked by inserting a skewer into the thickest part of the leg. The juices should run clear without a trace of pink.

Casseroling

Casseroling, otherwise known as braising, is an easy-to-learn culinary technique in which the meat, vegetables, seasonings and cooking liquid are gently simmered in the oven or over the lowest possible heat in a deep pan or casserole dish with a close-fitting lid. Rice, pasta or plainly boiled potatoes are the classic accompaniment. The technique is particularly delectable with chicken and is a good method for cooking larger, mature birds as it tenderizes the meat and the cooking juices can be reduced to make a wonderful sauce. The chicken is usually jointed, although small birds can be cooked whole if you have a deep enough pot. Season the chicken and brown all over in butter or hot oil, or a mixture of both. Pour in the liquid, which might be stock, wine or water, or a mixture of these, together with the other ingredients. Cover and simmer gently on top of the stove or in the oven for about 1 hour until the chicken is meltingly tender.

STARTERS & SNACKS

Infinitely versatile, cold chicken is the ideal standby for delicious and imaginative starters. Brought to life with oriental dressings or tropical fruits, chicken salad makes the perfect light lunch for the calorie conscious, or an appetizing starter. Chicken livers and dark leg meat can be turned into richly flavoured pâtés and potted meats to serve as a starter or to use as picnic material. When it comes to sandwiches, it's hard to beat a triple decker chicken club sandwich, although Middle Eastern pitta bread stuffed with spicy chicken and salad also hits the spot. Tender and moist, cooked chicken is a universal ingredient in countless snacks from all over the world.

CHICKEN IN PITTA BREAD (PAGE 18)

ORIENTAL CHICKEN SALAD

Mirin, soy sauce and sesame oil give an oriental flavour to this delicious salad.

SERVES 4

INGREDIENTS:
4 skinless, boneless chicken breasts
75 ml/3 fl oz/¹⁄₃ cup mirin or sweet sherry
75 ml/3 fl oz/¹⁄₃ cup light soy sauce
1 tbsp sesame oil
3 tbsp olive oil
1 tbsp red wine vinegar
1 tbsp Dijon mustard
250 g/8 oz egg noodles
250 g/8 oz bean-sprouts
250 g/8 oz Chinese leaves, shredded
2 spring onions (scallions), sliced
125 g/4 oz mushrooms, sliced

1 Pound the chicken breasts out to an even thickness between two sheets of clingfilm (plastic wrap) with a rolling pin or cleaver.

2 ▲ Put the chicken in a roasting tin (pan). Combine the mirin and soy sauce and brush the mixture over the chicken. Place in a preheated oven, 200°C/400°F/Gas Mark 6, for 20–30 minutes, basting often. Remove from the oven and allow to cool slightly.

3 ▼ Meanwhile, combine the oils and vinegar with the mustard.

4 ▼ Cook the noodles. Rinse under cold running water, then drain and immediately toss in the dressing.

5 ▼ Toss the bean-sprouts, Chinese leaves, spring onions (scallions) and mushrooms with the noodles.

6 Slice the cooked chicken very thinly and stir into the noodles. Serve the salad immediately.

CHICKEN, PAPAYA & AVOCADO SALAD

Try this recipe with peaches or nectarines instead of papaya.

SERVES 4

INGREDIENTS:
4 skinless, boneless chicken breasts
1 red chilli, deseeded and chopped
25 ml/1 fl oz/1²/₃ tbsps red wine vinegar
75 ml/3 fl oz/¹/₃ cup olive oil
1 papaya, peeled
1 avocado, peeled
125 g/4 oz alfalfa sprouts
125 g/4 oz bean-sprouts
salt and pepper

1 ▼ Poach the chicken breasts in boiling water for 15 minutes or until cooked through. Remove with a slotted spoon and set aside to cool.

2 ▼ Combine the chilli, vinegar and oil, season well and set aside.

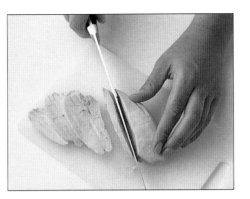

3 ▲ Place the chicken breasts on a chopping board. Using a very sharp knife, cut the chicken breasts across the grain into thin diagonal slices. Set aside.

4 ▼ Slice the papaya and avocado to the same thickness as the chicken. Arrange on four plates with the chicken, alfalfa sprouts and bean-sprouts. Serve with the dressing.

VERONICA SALAD

A delicious salad consisting of strips of cooked chicken with grapes, celery and hard-boiled (hard-cooked) eggs in a lightly curried, minty dressing garnished with chicory (endive).

SERVES 6

🐑🐑🐑🐑🐑🐑🐑🐑🐑🐑🐑🐑🐑🐑🐑

INGREDIENTS:
4 skinless, boneless chicken breasts
2 tbsp olive oil
1 tbsp sunflower oil
1–2 garlic cloves, crushed
1 onion, chopped finely
2 tbsp chopped fresh mint
4 green celery stalks
175 g/6 oz/1¹/₂ cups black grapes, preferably seedless
125 g/4 oz/1 cup large white (green) seedless grapes
30 g/1 oz/2 tbsp butter or margarine
1 tbsp plain (all-purpose) flour
¹/₂ tsp curry powder
3 tbsp white wine or stock
5 tbsp milk
2 tbsp natural fromage frais
2 tbsp mayonnaise
1 head chicory (endive)
2 hard-boiled (hard-cooked) eggs
salt and pepper

🐑🐑🐑🐑🐑🐑🐑🐑🐑🐑🐑🐑🐑🐑🐑

1 ▼ Cut the chicken into narrow strips. Heat the oils in a frying pan (skillet), add the garlic and chicken, and fry gently until well sealed. Add the onion and fry until the chicken and onion are tender. Stir in the mint and add salt and pepper. Drain off the oil and juices. Put the chicken mixture into a bowl and leave until cold.

2 ▲ Cut the celery into thin diagonal slices. Reserve a few whole black grapes for garnish. If they are large or contain pips (seeds), cut the remainder in half, remove any pips (seeds) and then add to the salad with the celery and the white (green) grapes.

3 Melt the butter or margarine in a pan, stir in the flour and curry powder, and cook for 1–2 minutes. Add the wine or stock and the milk, bring to the boil, simmering until thick. Remove from the heat, season, and stir in the fromage frais. Cover with clingfilm (plastic wrap) and leave until cold.

4 ▼ Stir the mayonnaise into the cold sauce and add to the chicken mixture, tossing to coat. Turn into a serving dish. Cut the chicory (endive) leaves into 5 cm/2 inch lengths and arrange around the edge of the salad with the reserved grapes and quarters of hard-boiled (hard-cooked) egg. Cover and chill until ready to serve.

CHICKEN PASTA PROVENCALE

Use any pasta shape for this salad, but drain thoroughly so that it does not dilute the dressing.

SERVES 4

INGREDIENTS:
175 g/6 oz dried pasta shapes
2 tbsp olive oil
350 g/12 oz skinless, boneless chicken
  breasts, cut into strips
2 courgettes (zucchini), sliced
1 red (bell) pepper, deseeded and cut
  into chunks
2 garlic cloves, sliced
4 tomatoes, cut into wedges
60 g/2 oz can of anchovies, drained
  and chopped
30 g/1 oz/¼ cup black olives, pitted
  and halved
sprig of fresh parsley, to garnish

FRENCH DRESSING:
3 tbsp olive oil
1 tbsp wine vinegar
1 garlic clove, crushed
½ tsp Dijon or Meaux mustard
1 tsp clear honey
salt and pepper

1 Cook the pasta in boiling salted water for 10–12 minutes until 'al dente'. Drain thoroughly.

2 Whisk all the dressing ingredients together until thoroughly blended.

3 ▲ Put the pasta into a bowl with 4 tablespoons of French dressing and mix together.

4 Heat the oil in a frying pan (skillet). Add the chicken and stir-fry for 4–5 minutes, stirring occasionally until cooked, then remove from the pan.

5 ▼ Add the courgettes (zucchini), (bell) pepper and garlic to the pan. Fry for 12–15 minutes, stirring, until softened.

6 ▲ Add the chicken, fried vegetables, tomatoes, anchovies and olives to the pasta and mix thoroughly together.

7 Transfer to a serving dish, garnish with parsley and serve immediately while warm.

CHICKEN LIVER & WATERCRESS PATE

The peppery flavours of the watercress really come through in this soft pâté – try serving it on hot melba toast as a delicious snack.

SERVES 4–6

INGREDIENTS:
60 g/2 oz/4 tbsp butter
1 onion, chopped
250 g/8 oz chicken livers
1 garlic clove, chopped
*125 g/4 oz watercress, trimmed and
    chopped*
1 tbsp chopped fresh thyme
1 tbsp chopped fresh parsley
1 tbsp sherry
salt and pepper
sprig of watercress, to garnish

1 ▼ Heat the butter in a frying pan (skillet) and fry the onion gently for about 5 minutes until soft.

2 ▼ Add the chicken livers and garlic and fry gently for 3–4 minutes until cooked through.

3 ▲ Set aside to cool slightly, before stirring in the watercress, fresh herbs, sherry and salt and pepper.

4 ▼ Transfer the mixture to a food processor and process until the chicken livers are finely chopped, but still have some texture – alternatively, put the mixture through a food mill.

5 Transfer the mixture to a serving dish. Cover and leave in the refrigerator to chill. Serve on hot melba toast.

POTTED CHICKEN

Cooked poultry, meat and game can all be prepared in this traditional way – finely minced (ground) and cooked with onions, spices and sherry or port. Serve as a first course or sandwich filling.

SERVES 4–6

INGREDIENTS:
250 g/8 oz boneless cooked chicken leg meat or any boneless game, beef or lamb
125 g/4 oz/$\frac{1}{2}$ cup butter
1 onion, chopped very finely
1–2 garlic cloves, crushed
2 tbsp sherry or port
about 4 tbsp stock
good pinch of ground mace, nutmeg or allspice
pinch of dried mixed herbs
salt and pepper
sprigs of fresh thyme, to garnish

TO SERVE:
sprigs of watercress
cherry tomatoes or tomato wedges
crusty bread or fingers of toast

1 ▼ Remove any skin and gristle from the poultry, game or meat. Finely mince (grind) twice, or finely chop in a food processor.

2 Melt half the butter in a saucepan and fry the onion and garlic gently until soft but only lightly coloured.

3 Stir the chicken into the pan, followed by the sherry or port and just enough of the stock to moisten the mixture. Season to taste with salt, pepper, mace and herbs.

4 ▲ Press the mixture into a lightly greased dish or several small individual dishes and level the top. Cover and chill until firm.

5 ▲ Melt the remaining butter and pour a thin layer over the potted chicken. Add a few sprigs of thyme and chill thoroughly so that the herbs set in the butter.

6 Serve spooned on to plates, or in individual pots on plates, garnished with watercress, tomatoes and crusty bread or fingers of toast.

CHICKEN IN PITTA BREAD

Pitta bread makes a great container for fast and flavoursome meals – either on the move or for a weekend lunch!

SERVES 4

INGREDIENTS:
1 tbsp cumin seed, crushed
1 tbsp coriander seed, crushed
1 tbsp ground turmeric
1 tbsp black mustard seed
2 tsp chilli flakes
50 ml/2 fl oz/¼ cup olive oil
750 g/1½ lb skinless, boneless chicken
300 ml/½ pint natural yogurt
90 g/3 oz fresh coriander (cilantro)
90 g/3 oz fresh mint
juice of 1 lime
sprig of flat-leaf parsley
salt and pepper

TO SERVE:
4 pitta breads
salad leaves (greens)
cucumber slices
cherry tomatoes

1 ▼ Combine the cumin, coriander, turmeric, mustard seed, chilli flakes and oil. Season generously with salt and pepper.

2 Cut the chicken into finger width strips and place in a large bowl. Toss in the spice mixture. Leave to marinate for 2 hours, or as long as possible.

3 Cook the chicken in a preheated oven, 220°C/425°F/Gas Mark 7, for 15 minutes, turning once or twice.

4 ▲ Meanwhile, make the yogurt chutney. Combine the yogurt and herbs in a food processor until smooth, or finely chop the herbs and stir into the yogurt. Add the lime juice and season well with salt and pepper. Place the yogurt chutney in a small bowl and garnish with a sprig of parsley.

5 ▼ To serve, split the pitta breads and warm them through. Stuff generously with salad leaves (greens), cucumber and tomatoes, and divide the chicken strips among them. Spoon over a little yogurt chutney and serve.

SUPER CLUB SANDWICH

Club sandwiches are intended to be more or less adequate substitutes for a full meal and can be as many layers high as you can manage!

SERVES 1

INGREDIENTS:
3 slices white or brown bread
60 g/2 oz/4 tbsp butter
125 g/4 oz cooked skinless, boneless
  chicken, shredded
3 tbsp lemon mayonnaise
4 small crisp lettuce leaves
1 tomato, sliced
5 cm/2 inch piece cucumber, sliced
salt and pepper

TO GARNISH:
sprigs of watercress
lemon wedges

1 Toast the slices of bread on both sides until golden, then spread each slice with butter.

2 ▲ In a small bowl, mix the chicken with the mayonnaise, and salt and pepper to taste.

3 Cover the first slice of toast with two of the lettuce leaves, then half of the chicken mixture and all of the tomato slices.

4 ▲ Cover with the second slice of toast, then the remaining chicken mixture and the sliced cucumber.

5 Place the third slice of toast on top, buttered side down, and press gently to seal.

6 ▼ With a sharp knife, cut the whole sandwich into two large triangles or alternatively into quarters, and secure each with a wooden cocktail stick (toothpick), if liked. Serve the sandwiches garnished with a sprig of watercress and a lemon wedge.

SPICED CHICKEN KOFTAS

Koftas are spicy balls of minced (ground) poultry or meat. Lime pickle is available in Asian food stores and some supermarkets.

SERVES 4

INGREDIENTS:

500 g/1 lb skinless, boneless chicken, chopped coarsely
1 garlic clove
2.5 cm/1 inch piece fresh ginger root, grated
1/2 green (bell) pepper, deseeded and chopped coarsely
2 fresh green chillies, deseeded and chopped
4 tsp garam masala
1/2 tsp ground turmeric
2 tbsp chopped fresh coriander (cilantro)
1/2 tsp salt
6 tbsp vegetable oil
1 jar lime pickle, to serve

TO GARNISH:

sprigs of coriander (cilantro)
lime wedges

1 Put all the ingredients except the oil and lime pickle into a food processor or blender and process until the mixture is chopped finely. Alternatively, chop the chicken, garlic, ginger, (bell) pepper and chillies very finely, and mix together in a bowl with the garam masala, turmeric, coriander (cilantro) and salt.

2 ▲ Shape the mixture with your hands to form 16 small balls.

3 ▼ Heat the oil in a wok or large frying pan (skillet) and fry the koftas for 8–10 minutes, turning occasionally. Fry in batches if necessary, keeping the first batch warm in a low oven.

4 ▲ Drain the koftas on paper towels and serve hot with lime pickle.

THAI CHICKEN SPRING ROLLS

A cucumber dipping sauce tastes perfect with these delicious spring rolls, filled with chicken and fresh, crunchy vegetables.

SERVES 4

INGREDIENTS:

1 tbsp light soy sauce
1 tsp sugar
2 tsp cornflour (cornstarch), blended with 2 tbsp cold water
2 tbsp vegetable oil
4 spring onions (scallions), trimmed and sliced very finely
1 carrot, cut into matchstick pieces
1 small green or red (bell) pepper, deseeded and sliced finely
60 g/2 oz/²/₃ cup button mushrooms, sliced
60 g/2 oz/1 cup bean-sprouts
175 g/6 oz/1 cup cooked skinless, boneless chicken, shredded
12 × 20 cm/8 inch spring roll wrappers
oil for deep-frying
salt and pepper
spring onion (scallion) brushes, to garnish

DIPPING SAUCE:

50 ml/2 fl oz/¹/₄ cup light malt vinegar
2 tbsp water
60 g/2 oz/¹/₄ cup light muscovado sugar
¹/₂ tsp salt
5 cm/2 inch piece of cucumber, peeled and chopped finely
4 spring onions (scallions), trimmed and sliced finely
1 small red or green chilli, deseeded and chopped very finely

1 Mix together the soy sauce, sugar and cornflour (cornstarch) paste.

2 Heat the oil in a wok or frying pan (skillet) and add the spring onions (scallions), carrot and (bell) pepper. Stir-fry for 2–3 minutes. Add the mushrooms, bean-sprouts and chicken and cook for a further 2 minutes. Season with salt and pepper.

3 Add the cornflour (cornstarch) mixture to the stir-fry and cook, stirring continuously for about 1 minute, until thickened. Leave to cool.

4 ▲ Place spoonfuls of the chicken mixture on to the spring roll wrappers. Dampen the edges and roll them up to enclose the filling completely.

5 ▲ To make the dipping sauce, heat the vinegar, water, sugar and salt in a saucepan. Boil for 1 minute. Mix the cucumber, spring onions (scallions) and chilli in a small serving bowl and pour over the vinegar mixture. Leave to cool.

6 Heat the oil and deep-fry the rolls until crisp and golden brown. Drain on paper towels, then serve, garnished with spring onion (scallion) brushes and accompanied by the cucumber dipping sauce.

CHICKEN SCALLOPS

Served in scallop shells, this dish makes a stylish presentation for a dinner-party first course.

SERVES 4

INGREDIENTS:

175 g/6 oz short-cut macaroni, or other
   short dried pasta shapes
3 tbsp vegetable oil, plus extra for
   brushing
1 onion, chopped finely
3 rashers unsmoked collar or back
   bacon, derinded and chopped
125 g/4 oz button mushrooms, sliced
   thinly
175 g/6 oz/³/₄ cup cooked skinless,
   boneless chicken, diced
175 ml/6 fl oz/³/₄ cup crème fraîche
4 tbsp dry breadcrumbs
60 g/2 oz/¹/₂ cup mature (sharp)
   Cheddar, grated
salt and pepper
sprigs of flat-leafed parsley, to garnish

1 Cook the pasta in a large pan of boiling salted water to which you have added 1 tablespoon of the oil. When the pasta is almost tender, drain in a colander, return to the pan and cover.

2 ▲ Heat the remaining oil in a pan over a medium heat and fry the onion until it is translucent. Add the chopped bacon and mushrooms and cook for a further 3–4 minutes, stirring once or twice.

3 Stir in the pasta, chicken and the crème fraîche and season to taste.

4 ▲ Brush four large scallop shells with oil. Spoon in the chicken mixture and smooth to make neat mounds.

5 ▼ Mix together the breadcrumbs and cheese, and sprinkle over the top of the shells. Press the topping lightly into the chicken mixture, and place under a preheated medium grill (broiler) for 4–5 minutes, until golden brown and bubbling. Garnish with parsley sprigs, and serve hot.

SOUPS

Laden with flavour and aroma, soup made with chicken must be the most comforting in the world. It produces a definite feeling of well-being which can help lift fatigue, and it's easy to digest but still satisfying. Chicken soup has long been heralded as a cure for countless illnesses known to man. For the best results, choose a boiling fowl or large roaster; young birds sold for frying have not yet developed the richness of flavour necessary for a satisfying soup. Most chicken soups benefit from a good quality home-made stock, although the better brands of stock cubes are fine in some cases. Every cuisine in the world has its favourite chicken soup recipe. In this chapter you'll find a selection from places as far afield as China, Mexico and Scotland. They are all delicious, easy to make and will guarantee success every time.

VEGETABLE & CHICK-PEA (GARBANZO BEAN) SOUP (PAGE 26)

CHICKEN & SWEETCORN SOUP

A hint of chilli and sherry flavour this chicken and sweetcorn soup which has both baby sweetcorn cobs and corn niblets in it, with red (bell) pepper and tomato for colour and flavour.

SERVES 4

INGREDIENTS:

1 skinless, boneless chicken breast, about 175 g/6 oz
2 tbsp sunflower oil
2–3 spring onions (scallions), thinly sliced diagonally
1 small or ½ large red (bell) pepper, cored, deseeded and thinly sliced
1 garlic clove, crushed
125 g/4 oz baby sweetcorn cobs, thinly sliced
1 litre/1¾ pints/4 cups chicken stock
200 g/7 oz can of sweetcorn niblets, well drained
2 tbsp sherry
2–3 tsp bottled sweet chilli sauce
2–3 tsp cornflour (cornstarch)
2 tomatoes, quartered and deseeded, then sliced
salt and pepper
chopped fresh coriander (cilantro) or parsley, to garnish

1 ▼ Cut the chicken breast into four strips lengthways, then cut each strip into narrow slices across the grain.

2 ▲ Heat the oil in a wok or large frying pan (skillet), swirling it around until it is really hot. Add the chicken and stir-fry for 3–4 minutes, moving it around the wok until it is well sealed all over and almost cooked through.

3 Add the spring onions (scallions), (bell) pepper and garlic to the wok, and continue to stir-fry for 2–3 minutes. Add the baby sweetcorn and stock and bring to the boil.

4 ▼ Add the sweetcorn niblets, sherry, sweet chilli sauce and salt to taste, and simmer for 5 minutes, stirring from time to time.

5 Blend the cornflour (cornstarch) with a little cold water. Add to the soup and bring to the boil. Add the tomato slices, adjust the seasoning and simmer for a few minutes. Serve the soup very hot, sprinkled with finely chopped coriander (cilantro) or parsley.

CHICKEN SOUP WITH ALMONDS

This soup can also be made using turkey or pheasant breasts. Pheasant gives a stronger, gamy flavour, particularly if game stock is made from the carcass and used in the soup.

SERVES 4

INGREDIENTS:
1 large or 2 small skinless, boneless
  chicken breasts
1 tbsp sunflower oil
1 carrot, cut into julienne strips
4 spring onions (scallions), thinly sliced
  diagonally
700 ml/1¼ pints/3 cups chicken stock
finely grated rind of ½ lemon
45 g/1½ oz/⅓ cup ground almonds
1 tbsp light soy sauce
1 tbsp lemon juice
30 g/1 oz/¼ cup flaked (slivered)
  almonds, toasted
salt and pepper
crusty bread, to serve

1 Cut each breast into four strips lengthways, then slice very thinly across the grain into shreds.

2 ▲ Heat the oil in the wok, swirling it around until really hot. Add the chicken and toss it in the oil for 3–4 minutes until sealed and almost cooked through. Add the carrot and continue cooking for 2–3 minutes, stirring all the time. Add the spring onions (scallions) and stir.

3 ▲ Add the stock to the wok and bring to the boil. Add the lemon rind, ground almonds, soy sauce and lemon juice and season with salt and pepper.

4 Bring back to the boil and simmer, uncovered, for 5 minutes, stirring from time to time.

5 Adjust the seasoning, add most of the toasted flaked (slivered) almonds and continue to cook for a further 1–2 minutes.

6 Serve the soup very hot, in individual bowls, sprinkled with the remaining almonds.

VEGETABLE & CHICK-PEA (GARBANZO BEAN) SOUP

A good tasty soup full of vegetables, chicken and chick-peas (garbanzo beans), with just a hint of spiciness, to serve on any occasion.

SERVES 4-6

INGREDIENTS:
3 tbsp olive oil
1 large onion, chopped finely
2–3 garlic cloves, crushed
$^{1}/_{2}$–1 red chilli, deseeded and chopped
   very finely
1 skinless, boneless chicken breast,
   about 150 g/5 oz, sliced thickly
2 celery stalks, chopped finely
175 g/6 oz carrots, grated coarsely
1.25 litres/2$^{1}/_{4}$ pints/6$^{1}/_{4}$ cups chicken stock
2 bay leaves
$^{1}/_{2}$ tsp dried oregano
$^{1}/_{4}$ tsp ground cinnamon
425 g/14 oz can of chick-peas
   (garbanzo beans), drained
250 g/8 oz tomatoes, peeled, deseeded
   and chopped
1 tbsp tomato purée (paste)
salt and pepper
chopped fresh coriander (cilantro) or
   parsley, to garnish
corn or wheat tortillas, to serve

1 Heat the oil in a large saucepan and fry the onion, garlic and chilli very gently until softened but not coloured.

2 ◣ Add the chicken to the saucepan and continue to cook until the chicken is well sealed.

3 ◣ Add the celery, carrots, stock, bay leaves, oregano, cinnamon, and salt and pepper. Bring to the boil, then cover and simmer gently for about 20 minutes, or until the chicken is tender.

4 ▼ Remove the chicken from the soup and chop it finely, or cut it into narrow strips.

5 Return the chicken to the pan with the chick-peas (garbanzo beans), tomatoes and tomato purée (paste). Simmer, covered, for a further 15–20 minutes. Discard the bay leaves, then adjust the seasoning.

6 Serve very hot sprinkled with coriander (cilantro) or parsley and accompanied by warmed tortillas.

COCK-A-LEEKIE SOUP

A traditional Scottish soup in which a whole chicken is cooked with the vegetables to add extra flavour to the stock. Add some of the cooked chicken to the soup and reserve the remainder for another meal.

SERVES 4–6

INGREDIENTS:

1–1.5 kg/2–3 lb oven-ready chicken
   plus giblets, if available
1.75–2 litres/3–3½ pints/8–9 cups
   chicken stock
1 onion, sliced thinly
4 leeks, sliced thinly
good pinch of ground allspice or
   ground coriander seeds
1 bouquet garni, (bay leaf, parsley and
   thyme sprigs, tied with string)
12 no-soak prunes, halved and pitted
salt and pepper
warm crusty bread, to serve

1 ▼ Put the chicken, giblets if using, stock and onion in a large saucepan. Bring to the boil and remove any scum from the surface using a perforated spoon.

2 ▼ Add the leeks, allspice or coriander, bouquet garni, and salt and pepper. Cover and simmer gently for 1½ hours until the chicken is falling off the bone.

3 Remove the chicken from the pan and skim any fat from the surface of the soup using a perforated spoon.

4 ▲ Chop some of the chicken flesh and return to the pan. Add the prunes, bring back to the boil and simmer, uncovered, for about 20 minutes.

5 Discard the bouquet garni, adjust the seasoning and serve.

CHICKEN & CHESTNUT SOUP

A rich soup based on a good stock with pieces of chicken and chopped chestnuts for an interesting flavour and texture.

SERVES 4–6

INGREDIENTS:

2 onions
1 raw or cooked chicken carcass, chopped, plus trimmings
chicken giblets, if available
1.5 litres/2½ pints/6¼ cups water
1 bouquet garni, (bay leaf, parsley and thyme sprigs, tied with string)
125 g/4 oz/½ cup fresh chestnuts, pierced and roasted for about 5 minutes or boiled for 30–40 minutes and drained, or 175 g/6 oz/1 cup canned peeled chestnuts
45 g/1½ oz/3 tbsp butter or margarine
45 g/1½ oz/⅓ cup plain (all-purpose) flour
150 ml/¼ pint/⅔ cup milk
½ tsp ground coriander seeds
90 g/3 oz/1½ cups carrots, grated coarsely
1 tbsp chopped fresh parsley (optional)
salt and pepper

1 ▼ Cut one of the onions into quarters. Put the chicken carcass, giblets if available, water, the quartered onion and bouquet garni into a saucepan. Bring to the boil, cover and simmer for about 1 hour, stirring occasionally.

2 Strain the stock and reserve 1 litre/1¾ pints/4 cups.

3 ▲ Remove 90–125 g/3–4 oz/½–¾ cup of chicken trimmings from the carcass and chop finely. If using canned chestnuts, drain well; if using fresh chestnuts, peel them. Finely chop the chestnuts. Chop the remaining onion.

4 Melt the butter or margarine in a saucepan and fry the onion gently until soft. Stir in the flour and cook for about 1 minute.

5 ▼ Gradually stir in the reserved stock and bring to the boil, stirring. Simmer for 2 minutes, then add the milk, coriander, chopped chicken, carrots, chestnuts, and salt and pepper.

6 Bring the soup back to the boil and simmer for 10 minutes, then stir in the parsley, if using. Adjust the seasoning before serving.

CHICKEN & SWEETCORN CHOWDER

A quick and satisfying soup, full of flavour and different textures.

SERVES 2

INGREDIENTS:
2 tsp oil
15 g/¹/₂ oz/1 tbsp butter or margarine
1 small onion, chopped finely
1 chicken quarter, 1 leg or 2–3
  drumsticks
1 tbsp plain (all-purpose) flour
600 ml/1 pint/2¹/₂ cups chicken stock
¹/₂ small red, yellow or orange (bell)
  pepper, deseeded and chopped finely
2 large tomatoes, peeled and chopped
2 tsp tomato purée (paste)
200 g/7 oz can of sweetcorn, drained
generous pinch of dried oregano
¹/₄ tsp ground coriander seeds
salt and pepper
chopped fresh parsley, to garnish
crusty bread, to serve

1 ▼ Heat the oil and butter or margarine in a saucepan and fry the onion gently until just beginning to soften. Cut the chicken quarter, if using, into two pieces. Add the chicken to the saucepan and fry until golden brown all over.

2 Add the flour and cook for 1–2 minutes. Then add the stock gradually, bring to the boil and simmer for about 5 minutes.

3 ▲ Add the (bell) pepper, tomatoes, tomato purée (paste), sweetcorn, oregano, coriander, and salt and pepper. Cover and simmer gently for about 20 minutes until the chicken is very tender.

4 ▲ Remove the chicken from the soup, strip the flesh from the bone and chop it finely with a sharp knife. Then return the chopped chicken to the soup.

5 Adjust the seasoning and simmer the soup for a further 2–3 minutes before sprinkling with chopped, fresh parsley. Serve the soup very hot with plenty of warm crusty bread.

NOODLES IN SOUP

Noodles in soup are popular in China. This is a thick, hearty soup. Add more stock if you prefer it thinner.

SERVES 4

INGREDIENTS:
250 g/8 oz cooked, skinless, boneless
  chicken
3–4 Chinese dried mushrooms, soaked
125 g/4 oz can of sliced bamboo shoots,
  rinsed and drained
125 g/4 oz spinach, lettuce hearts, or
  Chinese leaves, shredded
2 spring onions (scallions), finely
  shredded
250 g/8 oz egg noodles
about 600 ml/1 pint/2½ cups chicken
  stock
2 tbsp light soy sauce
2 tbsp vegetable oil
1 tsp salt
½ tsp sugar
2 tsp Chinese rice wine or dry sherry
a few drops of sesame oil
1 tsp red chilli oil (optional)

1 Cut the chicken into thin shreds. Squeeze dry the soaked mushrooms and discard the hard stalk.

2 ▲ Thinly shred the mushrooms, bamboo shoots, spinach and spring onions (scallions).

3 Cook the noodles in boiling water according to the instructions on the packet, then drain and rinse under cold water. Place the noodles in a bowl and set aside.

4 Bring the stock to the boil, add about 1 tablespoon of soy sauce and pour over the noodles. Keep warm.

5 ▲ Heat the oil in a heavy frying pan (skillet), add about half of the spring onions (scallions), the chicken, mushrooms, bamboo shoots and greens. Stir-fry for 2–3 minutes. Add the seasonings and blend together well.

6 ▼ Pour the mixture over the noodles, garnish with the remaining spring onions (scallions) and serve.

HOT & SOUR SOUP

This is one of the most popular soups in Chinese restaurants throughout the world.

SERVES 4

INGREDIENTS:
4–6 dried Chinese mushrooms
    (shiitake), soaked
125 g/4 oz cooked chicken (or pork)
1 cake tofu (bean curd)
60 g/2 oz can of sliced bamboo shoots,
    drained
1 tbsp cornflour (cornstarch)
600 ml/1 pint/2½ cups chicken stock
    or water
1 tbsp Chinese rice wine or dry sherry
1 tbsp light soy sauce
2 tbsp rice vinegar
½ tsp ground white pepper
salt
2–3 spring onions (scallions), thinly
    sliced, to garnish

1 Drain the mushrooms, squeeze dry and discard the hard stalks. Thinly slice the mushrooms.

2 ▲ Thinly slice the chicken, tofu (bean curd) and bamboo shoots into narrow shreds using a cleaver.

3 Mix the cornflour (cornstarch) with 1½ tablespoons of water to form a paste and set aside.

4 ▼ Bring the stock or water to a rolling boil in a wok or large frying pan (skillet) and add the mushrooms, chicken, tofu (bean curd) and bamboo shoots. Bring back to the boil then simmer for about 1 minute.

5 ▲ Add the wine, soy sauce and vinegar. Bring back to the boil, stirring in the cornflour (cornstarch) paste. Add the pepper and season with salt to taste. Serve hot, sprinkled with the spring onions (scallions).

CHICKEN & NOODLE ONE-POT

Flavoursome chicken and vegetables cooked with Chinese egg noodles in a coconut sauce. Increase the amount of stock for a thinner soup. Serve in deep soup bowls.

SERVES 4

INGREDIENTS:

1 tbsp sunflower oil
1 onion, sliced
1 garlic clove, crushed
2.5 cm/1 inch fresh ginger root, grated
1 bunch spring onions (scallions), sliced diagonally
500 g/1 lb skinless, boneless chicken breasts, cut into bite-sized pieces
2 tbsp mild curry paste
500 ml/16 fl oz/2 cups coconut milk
300 ml/½ pint/1¼ cups chicken stock
250 g/8 oz Chinese egg noodles
2 tsp lime juice
salt and pepper
sprigs of basil, to garnish

1 Heat the oil in a wok or large, heavy-based frying pan (skillet). Add the onion, garlic, ginger and spring onions (scallions) and stir-fry for 2 minutes until softened.

2 ▲ Add the chicken pieces and curry paste. Stir-fry for about 4 minutes until the vegetables and chicken are golden brown.

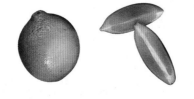

3 ▼ Stir in the coconut milk, stock, and salt and pepper to taste, mixing until well blended. Bring to the boil.

4 ▼ Break the noodles into large pieces, if necessary, and add to the pan. Cover and simmer for about 6–8 minutes, stirring occasionally, until the noodles are just tender.

5 Add the lime juice, adjust the seasoning and garnish with basil sprigs. Serve at once in deep soup bowls.

LIGHT MEALS

A tasty but well-made light meal is the answer to today's hectic lifestyle. Family members may want to eat at different times and many of us are too busy to prepare or eat a traditional three-course meal every day. Chicken is the perfect ingredient for a light meal. It's high in protein and B vitamins, and low in fat, so your diet will not suffer if you skip a full-scale meal now and then. Chicken can be cooked in countless ways and happily partners so many different flavours that you'll find it hard to run out of ideas. The selection in this chapter ranges from simple dishes such as Pasta Medley to the more unusual Bang Bang Chicken from China. There are also some Mexican favourites such as Chicken Fajitas, as well as recipes for traditional chicken pies – delicious with pickles and a salad.

SPICED CHICKEN & GRAPE SALAD

Tender chicken breasts, sweet grapes and crisp celery coated in a mild curry mayonnaise make a wonderful al fresco lunch.

SERVES 4

INGREDIENTS:
500 g/1 lb cooked skinless, boneless chicken breasts
2 celery stalks, sliced finely
250 g/8 oz/2 cups black grapes
60 g/2 oz/$^1/_2$ cup split almonds, toasted
pinch of paprika
sprigs of fresh coriander (cilantro) or flat-leafed parsley, to garnish

CURRY SAUCE:
150 ml/$^1/_4$ pint/$^2/_3$ cup mayonnaise
125 g/4 oz/$^1/_2$ cup natural fromage frais
1 tbsp clear honey
1 tbsp curry paste

1 ▼ Cut the chicken into fairly large pieces and put in a bowl with the celery.

2 ▼ Halve the grapes, remove the seeds and add to the chicken and celery.

3 ▼ To make the curry sauce, mix the mayonnaise, fromage frais, honey and curry paste together until blended.

4 ▲ Pour the curry sauce over the salad and mix together carefully until well coated.

5 Transfer to a shallow serving dish and sprinkle with the almonds and paprika. Garnish with the coriander (cilantro) or parsley.

CHICKEN WITH LEMON & TARRAGON

Chicken fillets are cooked with saffron, white wine and stock flavoured with lemon rind and tarragon, then the sauce is thickened with egg yolks and soured cream and finished with mayonnaise.

SERVES 6

INGREDIENTS:
6 large skinless, boneless chicken breasts
¼ tsp saffron strands
250 ml/8 fl oz/1 cup boiling water
1 tbsp olive oil
30 g/1 oz/2 tbsp butter
1 garlic clove, crushed
120 ml/4 fl oz/½ cup dry white wine
grated rind of 1 small lemon
1 tbsp lemon juice
1–2 tbsp chopped fresh tarragon
2 tsp cornflour (cornstarch)
1 egg yolk
6 tbsp soured cream or double (heavy) cream
4 tbsp thick mayonnaise
salt and pepper

TO GARNISH:
sprigs of fresh tarragon
lemon twists

1 ▼ Cut each chicken breast almost horizontally into three thin slices with a sharp knife. Season each piece well with salt and pepper.

2 Put the saffron strands into a bowl, pour on the boiling water and leave to stand until needed.

3 Heat the oil, butter and garlic in a frying pan (skillet). When foaming, add the chicken and fry on each side until lightly coloured.

4 ▲ Add the saffron solution, wine, half the tarragon and the lemon rind and juice. Bring to the boil, then simmer for about 5 minutes until tender.

5 Remove the chicken pieces with a perforated spoon and place on a serving dish in overlapping slices. Leave to cool. Boil the remaining juices in the pan for 3–4 minutes to reduce slightly.

6 Blend the cornflour (cornstarch), egg yolk and cream together in a bowl. Whisk in a little of the cooking juices, then return to the pan and heat gently, stirring continuously until thickened and just barely simmering. Remove from the heat, adjust the seasoning and pour into a bowl. Cover and leave until cool.

7 ▼ Beat the mayonnaise and remaining fresh tarragon into the sauce and spoon over the chicken. Cover and chill thoroughly. Garnish with sprigs of fresh tarragon and lemon twists.

BANG-BANG CHICKEN

The cooked chicken meat is tenderized by being pounded with a rolling pin, hence the name for this very popular dish from Szechuan in China.

SERVES 4

INGREDIENTS:
1 litre/1¾ pints/4 cups water
2 chicken quarters (breast and leg)
1 cucumber, cut into matchstick shreds

SAUCE:
2 tbsp light soy sauce
1 tsp sugar
1 tbsp finely chopped spring onion
   (scallion)
1 tsp red chilli oil
¼ tsp pepper
1 tsp white sesame seeds
2 tbsp peanut butter, creamed with a
   little sesame oil

1 ▼ Bring the water to a rolling boil in a large saucepan or a wok. Add the chicken pieces, reduce the heat, cover and cook for 30–35 minutes.

2 ▼ Remove the chicken from the pan and immerse it in a bowl of cold water for at least 1 hour to cool it, ready for shredding.

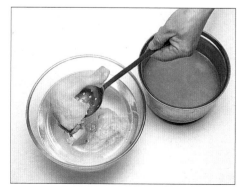

3 Remove the chicken pieces with a perforated spoon and drain well. Pat dry with paper towels, then strip the meat from the bone.

4 ▲ On a flat surface, pound the chicken with a rolling pin, then tear the meat into shreds with two forks. Mix with the shredded cucumber and arrange in a serving dish.

5 To serve, mix together all the sauce ingredients and pour over the chicken and cucumber.

THAI-STYLE CHICKEN FRIED RICE

A few authentic ingredients give this spicy fried rice dish a typically Thai flavour.

SERVES 4

INGREDIENTS:

250 g/8 oz/1¼ cups white long-grain rice
4 tbsp vegetable oil
2 garlic cloves, chopped finely
6 shallots, sliced finely
1 red (bell) pepper, deseeded and diced
125 g/4 oz French (green) beans, cut into 2.5 cm/1 inch lengths
1 tbsp Thai red curry paste
350 g/12 oz cooked skinless, boneless chicken, chopped
½ tsp ground coriander seeds
1 tsp finely grated fresh ginger root
2 tbsp Thai fish sauce
finely grated rind of 1 lime
3 tbsp lime juice
1 tbsp chopped fresh coriander (cilantro)
salt and pepper

TO GARNISH:
lime wedges
sprigs of fresh coriander (cilantro)

1 Cook the rice in boiling, lightly salted water for 12–15 minutes until tender. Drain, rinse in cold water and drain again thoroughly.

2 ▼ Heat the oil in a large frying pan (skillet) or wok and add the garlic and shallots. Fry gently for 2–3 minutes until golden.

3 ▼ Add the (bell) pepper and French (green) beans and stir-fry for 2 minutes. Add the Thai curry paste and stir-fry for 1 minute.

4 ▲ Add the cooked rice to the pan, then the chicken, ground coriander seeds, ginger, fish sauce, lime rind and juice, and fresh coriander (cilantro). Stir-fry over a medium-high heat for 4–5 minutes, until the rice and chicken are thoroughly reheated. Season to taste.

5 Garnish with lime wedges and coriander (cilantro) before serving.

CRUNCHY-TOPPED CHICKEN/SPICED CHICKEN SALAD

Cook four chicken pieces together, and serve two hot, topped with a crunchy herb mixture and white sauce, accompanied by potatoes or pasta. Then mix the remaining ingredients with grapes and a delicious curry sauce to make a spicy chicken salad.

SERVES 2

INGREDIENTS:

4 chicken thighs
oil for brushing
garlic powder
½ dessert (eating) apple, grated coarsely
1½ tbsp dry parsley and thyme stuffing mix
salt and pepper
pasta shapes, to serve

SAUCE:

15 g/½ oz/1 tbsp butter or margarine
2 tsp plain (all-purpose) flour
5 tbsp milk
2 tbsp dry white wine or stock
½ tsp dried mustard powder
1 tsp capers or chopped gherkins
salt and pepper

SPICED CHICKEN SALAD:

½ small onion, chopped finely
1 tbsp oil
1 tsp tomato purée (paste)
½ tsp curry powder
1 tsp apricot jam
1 tsp lemon juice
2 tbsp mayonnaise
1 tbsp soured cream or natural fromage frais
90 g/3 oz/¾ cup seedless grapes, halved
salt and pepper
60 g/2 oz/¼ cup white long-grain rice, cooked, to serve

1 Place the chicken in a shallow ovenproof dish. Brush with oil, sprinkle with garlic powder and season with salt and pepper. Place in a preheated oven, 200°C/400°F/Gas Mark 6, for 25 minutes, or until almost cooked through.

2 ▼ Combine the apple with the stuffing mix. Baste the chicken, then spoon the mixture over two of the pieces. Return all the chicken pieces to the oven for about 10 minutes until the chicken is cooked.

3 To make the sauce, melt the butter or magarine in a pan, stir in the flour and cook for 1–2 minutes. Add the milk gradually, then the wine or stock, and bring to the boil. Stir in the mustard, capers or gherkins, and seasoning. Simmer for 1 minute. Serve the two crunchy-topped pieces of chicken with the sauce and pasta shapes.

4 For the salad, fry the onion gently in the oil until barely coloured. Add the tomato purée (paste), curry powder and jam, and cook for 1 minute. Leave the mixture to cool.

5 Blend the mixture in a food processor, or press through a sieve (strainer). Beat in the lemon juice, mayonnaise and soured cream or fromage frais. Season to taste with salt and pepper.

6 ▼ Cut the chicken into strips and add to the sauce together with the grapes. Mix well, and chill for at least 2 hours. Serve with the rice.

CHICKEN & HAM PIE

Made with yogurt shortcrust pastry, this pie has a really moist filling and a melt-in-the-mouth crust.

SERVES 6

INGREDIENTS:
60 g/2 oz/4 tbsp butter
*30 g/1 oz/¼ cup plain (all-purpose)
   flour*
150 ml/¼ pint/⅔ cup milk
150 ml/¼ pint/⅔ cup natural yogurt
2 small leeks, sliced
*250 g/8 oz skinless, boneless chicken
   breasts, finely diced*
250 g/8 oz ham, diced
1 tsp soy sauce
pepper
dill sprigs, to garnish

PASTRY:
*250 g/8 oz/2 cups plain (all-purpose)
   flour, plus extra for dusting*
½ tsp mustard powder
¼ tsp salt
175 g/6 oz/¾ cup butter, diced
about 3 tbsp natural yogurt
2 tbsp milk to glaze

1 ▽ To make the pastry, grease a loose-bottomed flan tin, 4 cm/1¾ inches deep. Sift together the flour, mustard powder and salt. Rub in the butter until the mixture resembles fine breadcrumbs. Stir in enough yogurt to make a firm and non-sticky dough. Wrap the dough in foil and chill.

2 Melt 30 g/1 oz/2 tablespoons of the butter in a pan over a medium heat. Blend in the flour then pour on the milk and yogurt, stirring all the time. Simmer, uncovered, for 5 minutes, then remove from the heat. Transfer the sauce to a bowl and leave to cool.

3 Melt the remaining butter in a pan and fry the leeks for 2–3 minutes.

4 ▲ Pour the white sauce over the leeks, add the chicken and ham, and cook for 5 minutes. Add the soy sauce and season with pepper, then leave to cool completely.

5 ▲ Roll out the pastry on a floured board. Use just over half of the pastry to line the prepared tin. Pour in the cold filling. Roll out the remaining pastry and cover the pie. Trim the edges and press together firmly. Brush the top with milk. Re-roll the trimmings and cut into decorative shapes. Arrange the shapes over the pie and brush with milk. Bake in a preheated oven, 200°C/400°F/Gas Mark 6, for 35 minutes, or until golden brown. Serve the pie hot or cold.

RAISED CHICKEN PIE

A filling of diced chicken leg meat, minced (ground) pork and bacon with pickled walnuts, mushrooms and herbs is enclosed in a hot-water pastry crust.

SERVES 6

INGREDIENTS:
350 g/12 oz skinless, boneless chicken thighs
125 g/4 oz/^{1}/$_2$ cup lean pork, minced (ground)
125 g/4 oz/^{1}/$_2$ cup cooked ham, minced (ground) coarsely or chopped finely
1 small onion, very finely chopped
60 g/2 oz/^{2}/$_3$ cup button mushrooms, chopped roughly
1 tbsp chopped fresh parsley
good pinch of ground coriander seeds
6 pickled walnuts, well drained
beaten egg or milk to glaze
1 tsp powdered gelatine
150 ml/^{1}/$_4$ pint/^{2}/$_3$ cup chicken stock
salt and pepper

PASTRY:
350 g/12 oz/3 cups plain (all-purpose) flour
1 tsp salt
90 g/3 oz/^{1}/$_3$ cup lard (shortening)
6 tbsp water
3 tbsp milk

1 To make the filling, chop the chicken thighs and mix with the pork, ham, onion, mushrooms, parsley, ground coriander, and salt and pepper.

2 To make the pastry, sift the flour and salt into a bowl. Put the lard (shortening) in a saucepan with the water and milk and heat until melted, then bring to the boil. Pour on to the flour and mix until an even dough is formed.

3 Roll out about three-quarters of the dough and use to line a lightly greased raised pie mould or a loaf tin.

4 ▲ Put half the chicken mixture into the lined tin and arrange the walnuts over it. Cover with the rest of the chicken mixture. Roll out the reserved pastry for a lid, dampen the edges and position. Trim and crimp the edge. Make a hole in the centre for steam to escape. Garnish with pastry leaves and glaze with beaten egg or milk.

5 Bake on a baking sheet (cookie sheet) in a preheated oven, 200°C/400°F/Gas Mark 6, for 30 minutes.

Reduce the temperature to 180°C/350°F/Gas Mark 4, glaze again and bake for 1 hour. When browned, cover with a sheet of baking parchment. Remove the pie from the oven and leave to cool for 10 minutes.

6 ▼ Dissolve the gelatine in the stock, bringing just to the boil, and season well. Gradually pour in as much stock as possible through the hole in the pastry lid. Leave until cold and then chill thoroughly for at least 12 hours. Unmould the pie before serving.

THREE FILLET PARCEL (PACKAGE)

Fillets of chicken, lamb and pork are layered with sage leaves, wrapped in spinach leaves, covered with a layer of cottage cheese and enclosed in puff pastry. This is delicious served cold and cut into slices.

SERVES 8

INGREDIENTS:
300–350 g/10–12 oz pork fillet or tenderloin
about 12 fresh sage leaves
250–300 g/8–10 oz lamb neck fillet
2 skinless, boneless chicken breasts, total weight about 300 g/10 oz
2 tbsp oil
125 g/4 oz large spinach leaves
350 g/12 oz puff pastry, thawed if frozen
250 g/8 oz/1 cup cottage cheese
pinch of ground allspice
pinch of garlic powder
beaten egg or milk to glaze
salt and pepper

TO GARNISH:
sprigs of sage
cucumber slices

1 ▼ Layer the fillets beginning with the pork fillet, cover with half the sage leaves, then add the lamb fillet, the rest of the sage leaves and finally the chicken fillets. Secure with fine string and/or skewers.

2 Heat the oil in a frying pan (skillet) and fry the layered fillets for about 15 minutes, turning until browned and partly cooked. Remove from the pan (skillet) and leave until cold.

3 Blanch the spinach leaves in boiling water for 2 minutes then drain them thoroughly.

4 ▼ Roll out the pastry thinly into a rectangle large enough to enclose the layered fillets and allow for five narrow strips to be cut off the edge. Cut off the strips, then lay the spinach down the centre of the pastry and spread with the cottage cheese. Season well with allspice, garlic powder, and salt and pepper.

5 ▼ Remove the string or skewers from the fillets and place on top of the cheese and spinach. Wrap up in the pastry, dampening the pastry edges to secure. Place on a greased baking sheet (cookie sheet) and glaze with beaten egg or milk. Lay the strips of pastry over the roll and glaze again.

6 Bake in a preheated oven, 200°C/400°F/Gas Mark 6, for 30 minutes until just beginning to brown. Then reduce the temperature to 180°C/350°F/Gas Mark 4 and bake for a further 20 minutes. Remove from the oven and leave to cool, then chill thoroughly. Serve in slices garnished with sage leaves and slices of cucumber.

CHICKEN & SWEETCORN PUFF

This delicious choux puff is an impressive dish yet it's simple to make. You can use the choux pastry as a topping for all kinds of fillings.

SERVES 4

INGREDIENTS:
30 g/1 oz/2 tbsp butter or margarine
30 g/1 oz/¼ cup plain (all-purpose) flour
300 ml/½ pint/1¼ cups skimmed milk
250 g/8 oz/1 cup skinless, boneless cooked chicken, shredded
125 g/4 oz can of sweetcorn, drained
1 tbsp chopped fresh parsley
salt and pepper

CHOUX PASTRY:
75 g/2½ oz/generous ½ cup plain (all-purpose) flour
60 g/2 oz/4 tbsp butter or margarine
150 ml/¼ pint/⅔ cup water
2 eggs, beaten
salt

1 ▼ To make the choux pastry, sift the flour and salt into a bowl. Put the butter or margarine and water into a pan, then heat gently until the butter has melted. Bring to the boil. Remove from the heat and add the flour all at once. Beat with a wooden spoon until the mixture leaves the sides of the pan clean. Leave to cool slightly.

2 Gradually beat in the eggs until the mixture is thick and very glossy. Chill while making the filling.

3 To make the filling, put the butter or margarine, flour and milk into a saucepan. Heat, whisking constantly, until smooth and thickened.

4 ▼ Add the chicken, sweetcorn and parsley to the sauce. Season to taste. Pour into a 1 litre/1¾ pint/4 cup shallow baking dish.

5 ▲ Spoon the choux pastry around the edge of the dish. Bake in a preheated oven, 220°C/425°F/Gas Mark 7, for 35–40 minutes until puffed up and golden brown. Serve at once.

TAGLIATELLE WITH CHICKEN & ALMONDS

Spinach tagliatelle covered with a rich tomato sauce and topped with creamy chicken makes an appetizing lunch or supper dish.

SERVES 4

INGREDIENTS:
60 g/2 oz/4 tbsp unsalted butter
425 g/14 oz skinless, boneless chicken
  breasts, sliced thinly
90 g/3 oz/³/₄ cup blanched almonds
300 ml/¹/₂ pint/1¹/₄ cups double (heavy)
  cream
250 g/8 oz fresh green ribbon noodles
salt and pepper
basil leaves, to garnish

TOMATO SAUCE:
1 small onion, chopped
2 tbsp olive oil
1 garlic clove, chopped
425 g/14 oz can of chopped tomatoes
2 tbsp chopped fresh parsley
1 tsp dried oregano
2 bay leaves
2 tbsp tomato purée (paste)
1 tsp sugar

1 ▼ To make the tomato sauce, fry the onion gently in the oil until translucent. Add the garlic and fry for 1 minute more until just golden. Stir in the remaining ingredients and bring to the boil. Simmer, uncovered, for 15–20 minutes until reduced by half. Discard the bay leaves and keep the sauce warm.

2 ▼ Melt the butter in a pan and fry the chicken and almonds gently for 5–6 minutes, stirring frequently.

3 Meanwhile, put the cream in a small pan and boil for about 10 minutes, until reduced by almost half.

4 ▼ Stir the cream into the chicken mixture and season with salt and pepper. Set aside and keep warm.

5 Cook the pasta in a large pan of boiling salted water until just tender. Drain the pasta well, then turn into a warmed serving dish.

6 Spoon the tomato sauce over the pasta with the chicken mixture on top. Garnish with basil and serve.

TORTELLINI

According to legend, tortellini are said to resemble Venus's tummy button.

SERVES 4

INGREDIENTS:
125 g/4 oz cooked skinless, boneless
  chicken breasts, chopped
60 g/2 oz Parma ham (prosciutto)
45 g/1½ oz cooked drained spinach
1 tbsp finely chopped onion
2 tbsp grated Parmesan
good pinch of ground allspice
1 egg, beaten
salt and pepper

PASTA DOUGH:
325 g/11 oz/generous 2½ cups flour
pinch of salt
3 large eggs
1 tbsp olive oil
1 tbsp water

SAUCE:
300 ml/½ pint/1¼ cups single
  (light) cream
1–2 garlic cloves, crushed
125 g/4 oz mushrooms, thinly sliced
4 tbsp freshly grated Parmesan
1–2 tbsp freshly chopped parsley
salt and pepper

1 ▲ To make the pasta dough, sift the flour and salt on to a flat surface. Make a well in the centre. Beat the eggs, oil and water together, and pour into the well. Work in the flour to form a dough. Knead for 10–15 minutes until smooth. Cover with a damp cloth and leave for 10–15 minutes.

2 Put the chicken into a food processor with the Parma ham (prosciutto), spinach and onion. Process until finely chopped. Add the Parmesan, allspice, seasonings and egg.

3 ▲ Roll out the dough, half at a time, as thinly as possible. Cut into 4–5 cm/ 1½–2 inch rounds. Place ½ teaspoon of the filling on each circle. Fold into a semi-circle, sealing the edges firmly. Wrap the semi-circle round your index finger, crossing the ends. Press firmly together. Curl the rest of the dough back to make a 'tummy button' shape. Remove from your finger and lay on a floured tray. Repeat with the rest of the dough, re-rolling the trimmings.

4 ▼ Bring a large pan of salted water to the boil and add the tortellini in batches. Once they rise to the surface, cook for about 5 minutes, giving an occasional stir. Remove with a perforated spoon and drain on paper towels. Keep warm in a serving dish while cooking the remainder.

5 To make the sauce, heat the cream with the garlic and bring to the boil; simmer for a few minutes. Add the mushrooms, half the Parmesan and seasoning and simmer for 2–3 minutes. Stir in the parsley and pour over the warm tortellini. Sprinkle with the remaining Parmesan and serve immediately.

PASTA MEDLEY

Strips of cooked chicken are tossed with coloured pasta, grapes and carrot sticks in a pesto-flavoured dressing. Any leftovers can be kept in the refrigerator for a day or two.

SERVES 2

INGREDIENTS:
*125–150 g/4–5 oz dried pasta shapes,
  such as twists or bows
1 tbsp oil
2 tbsp mayonnaise
2 tsp bottled pesto sauce
1 tbsp soured cream or natural
  fromage frais
175 g/6 oz cooked skinless, boneless
  chicken meat
1–2 celery stalks
125 g/4 oz/1 cup black grapes
  (preferably seedless)
1 large carrot, trimmed
salt and pepper
celery leaves, to garnish*

FRENCH DRESSING:
*1 tbsp wine vinegar
3 tbsp extra-virgin olive oil
salt and pepper*

1 To make the French dressing, whisk all the ingredients together until smooth.

2 ▼ Cook the pasta with the oil for about 12 minutes in plenty of boiling salted water until just tender. Drain thoroughly, rinse and drain again. Transfer to a bowl and mix in 1 tablespoon of the French dressing while hot; leave until cold.

3 Combine the mayonnaise, pesto sauce and soured cream or fromage frais in a bowl, and season to taste.

4 ▲ Cut the chicken into narrow strips. Cut the celery diagonally into narrow slices. Reserve a few grapes for garnish, halve the rest and remove any pips (seeds). Cut the carrot into narrow julienne strips.

5 ▼ Add the chicken, the celery, the halved grapes, the carrot and the mayonnaise mixture to the pasta, and toss thoroughly. Check the seasoning, adding more salt and pepper if necessary.

6 Arrange the pasta mixture on two plates and garnish with the reserved black grapes and the celery leaves.

CHICKEN FAJITAS

This spicy chicken filling, made with mixed (bell) peppers, chillies and mushrooms and strongly flavoured with lime, is served in folded tortillas and topped with soured cream, sliced red onion, chopped tomato and lime wedges. Many other fillings can be used – the possibilities are endless.

SERVES 4

INGREDIENTS:
2 red (bell) peppers
2 green (bell) peppers
2 tbsp olive oil
2 onions, chopped
3 garlic cloves, crushed
1 chilli, deseeded and chopped finely
2 skinless, boneless chicken breasts,
  about 350 g/12 oz
60 g/2 oz button mushrooms, sliced
2 tsp chopped fresh coriander (cilantro)
grated rind of ¹/₂ lime
2 tbsp lime juice
4 wheat or corn tortillas
4–6 tbsp soured cream
salt and pepper

TO GARNISH:
sliced red onion
chopped tomatoes
lime wedges

1 ▼ Halve the (bell) peppers, remove the seeds and place skin-side upwards under a preheated moderate grill (broiler) until well charred. Leave to cool slightly and then peel off the skin. Cut the flesh into thin slices.

2 Heat the oil in a pan, add the onions, garlic and chilli, and fry gently for a few minutes until the onion has softened.

3 ▲ Cut the chicken into narrow strips. Add to the vegetable mixture in the pan and fry for 4–5 minutes until almost cooked, stirring occasionally.

4 Add the peppers, mushrooms, coriander (cilantro), lime rind and juice, and continue to cook for 2–3 minutes. Season to taste.

5 ▲ Heat the tortillas, wrapped in foil, in a preheated oven, 180°C/350°F/ Gas Mark 4, for 4–5 minutes. Bend them in half and divide the chicken mixture between them.

6 Top the chicken filling with soured cream and serve garnished with red onion slices, chopped tomatoes and lime wedges.

ENCHILADA LAYERS

You can vary the filling for these layered Mexican tortillas by using beef, fish or shellfish. If preferred, the tortillas can be rolled up once they are filled, rather than baking them in layers.

SERVES 4

INGREDIENTS:
500 g/1 lb skinless, boneless chicken breasts
2 tbsp olive oil
1 large onion, sliced thinly
3 garlic cloves, crushed
1 tsp ground cumin seeds
2 tbsp stock or water
1 tbsp chopped fresh coriander (cilantro)
6 wheat or corn tortillas
175 g/6 oz Feta cheese or white Cheshire cheese, coarsely grated
salt and pepper
sprigs of fresh coriander (cilantro), to garnish

TOMATO SAUCE:
2 tbsp oil
1 onion, chopped very finely
3 garlic cloves, crushed
1 red chilli, deseeded and chopped finely
425 g/14 oz can of chopped tomatoes with herbs
200 g/7 oz can of peeled tomatoes, chopped
3 tbsp tomato purée (paste)
2 tbsp lime juice
2 tsp caster (superfine) sugar
salt and pepper

1 Chop the chicken flesh finely. Heat the oil in a pan and fry the onion and garlic gently until softened.

2 ▲ Add the chicken and fry, stirring, for about 5 minutes until well sealed and almost cooked. Add the cumin, stock or water, and salt and pepper. Continue to cook for 2–3 minutes until tender, then stir in the coriander (cilantro). Remove from the heat.

3 To make the tomato sauce, heat the oil in a pan and fry the onion, garlic and chilli gently until softened.

4 Add both cans of tomatoes, the tomato purée (paste), lime juice, sugar and seasoning. Bring to the boil and simmer gently for 10 minutes.

5 ▼ Place a tortilla on a greased ovenproof dish, cover with a fifth of the chicken mixture and 2 tablespoons of the tomato sauce, then sprinkle over a layer of the grated cheese. Continue to layer in this way, finishing with a tortilla, the remaining tomato sauce and cheese.

6 Place uncovered, in a preheated oven, 190°C/375°F/Gas Mark 5, for about 25 minutes, or until the top is lightly browned and bubbling. Serve the enchiladas cut into wedges and garnished with a sprig of coriander (cilantro).

CHICKEN BURRITOS

A filling of chopped chicken and scrambled eggs, together with sliced tomatoes and a spicy pumpkin seed, herb and yogurt mixture, is rolled into wheat or corn tortillas.

SERVES 4

INGREDIENTS:
60 g/2 oz pumpkin seeds
3–4 spring onions (scallions), trimmed and sliced
1 chilli, deseeded and chopped finely
4 tbsp chopped fresh flat-leafed parsley
1 tbsp chopped fresh coriander (cilantro)
6 tbsp natural yogurt
4 wheat or corn tortillas
30 g/1 oz/2 tbsp butter
4 tbsp milk
1 garlic clove, crushed
6 eggs, beaten lightly
125 g/4 oz cooked skinless, boneless chicken, shredded
2 tomatoes, peeled and sliced
salt and pepper

TO GARNISH:
shredded lettuce
sliced red onions
chopped tomatoes

1 ▼ Toast the pumpkin seeds lightly in a heavy-based frying pan (skillet) with no added fat. Chop finely, then put into a food processor with the spring onions (scallions) and chilli and work until well blended. Alternatively, chop the spring onions (scallions) very finely and pound with the seeds and chilli using a pestle and mortar.

2 ▲ Add the chopped parsley and coriander (cilantro), followed by the yogurt, and blend until well mixed. Season to taste with salt and pepper.

3 Wrap the tortillas in foil and warm in a preheated oven, 180°C/350°F/Gas Mark 4, for 4–5 minutes.

4 Melt the butter with the milk, garlic, and salt and pepper. Remove from the heat and stir in the eggs. Cook over a gentle heat, stirring, until just scrambled. Stir in the cooked chicken.

5 ▼ Lay the tortillas flat and spoon the scrambled egg down the centre of each tortilla. Top with the pumpkin seed mixture and the tomatoes.

6 Roll up the tortillas and serve garnished with the shredded lettuce, sliced red onions and chopped tomatoes.

SAUTES & STIR-FRIES

Tender and succulent, smaller cuts of chicken are perfect for sautés and stir-fries. Both frying techniques are universally used throughout the world and are easy to master. They form the basis of a limitless number of dishes ranging from the classic Chicken Kiev to stir-fried Chinese Chicken with Noodles. The direct heat transmitted from the pan sears the surface of the meat and seals in the juices so that the flesh retains moisture and flavour. If you're sautéing chicken with skin, cook the skin side thoroughly to render the fat and create a crispy texture. If you're stir-frying, cut the chicken into small equal-sized cubes or strips so that they cook evenly. Whichever method you choose, you can be sure of quickly cooked, mouthwatering meals every time.

CHICKEN, CORIANDER (CILANTRO), GINGER & LEMON STIR-FRY (PAGE 54)

CHICKEN KIEV

This classic dish from the Ukraine is delicious served with sautéd potatoes.

SERVES 4

INGREDIENTS:
1 garlic clove, crushed
90 g/3 oz/6 tbsp butter
4 skinless, boneless chicken breasts
2 eggs, beaten
2 tbsp milk
oil for deep frying
125 g/4 oz/1 cup plain (all-purpose) flour
fresh breadcrumbs, for coating
salt and pepper

TO GARNISH:
chopped parsley
lemon slices

1 ▼ Mash the garlic into the butter with a fork. Season and shape into a square pattie. Chill in the freezer.

2 ▼ Slice each chicken breast in half horizontally, and lay between sheets of clingfilm (plastic wrap). Flatten to an even thickness. Cover and chill.

3 ▼ When the butter is quite hard, cut it into four batons. Place a baton lengthways on four of the chicken pieces. Place another chicken piece on top then cover and chill until ready to serve.

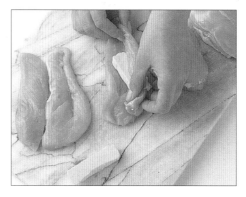

4 Beat the eggs and milk together. When ready to serve, heat the oil to moderate deep-frying temperature, 190°C/375°F, to a depth of about 5 cm/2 inches. Coat each Kiev with flour, then the egg mixture, and finally the breadcrumbs. Repeat once more to form a good seal. Fry each Kiev for about 5 minutes. Serve immediately, accompanied by sautéd potatoes and garnished with chopped parsley and lemon slices.

PAN-COOKED CHICKEN WITH ARTICHOKES

Artichokes are a familiar ingredient in Italian cookery. In this dish, they are used as a delicate flavouring.

SERVES 4

INGREDIENTS:
4 chicken breasts, part boned
2 tbsp olive oil
30 g/1 oz/2 tbsp butter
2 red onions, cut into wedges
2 tbsp lemon juice
150 ml/¼ pt/⅔ cup dry white wine
150 ml/¼ pt/⅔ cup chicken stock
2 tsp plain (all-purpose) flour
425 g/14 oz can of artichokes,
    drained and halved
salt and pepper
chopped fresh parsley, to garnish

1 ▼ Season the chicken with salt and freshly ground black pepper. Heat the oil and 15 g/½ oz/1 tablespoon of the butter in a large frying pan (skillet). Add the chicken and fry gently for 4–5 minutes on each side until lightly golden. Remove from the pan using a perforated spoon.

2 Toss the onion in the lemon juice, and add to the frying pan (skillet). Gently fry, stirring, for 3–4 minutes until just beginning to soften.

3 ▼ Return the chicken to the pan. Pour in the wine and stock, bring to the boil, then cover and simmer gently for 30 minutes.

4 Remove the chicken from the pan, reserving the cooking juices. Put in a serving dish and keep warm. Bring the pan juices to the boil, and boil rapidly for 5 minutes.

5 Blend the remaining butter with the flour to form a paste. Reduce the pan juices to a simmer and add the paste to the frying pan (skillet), stirring until thickened.

6 ▼ Adjust the seasoning, stir in the artichokes and cook for a further 2 minutes. Pour over the chicken and garnish with parsley.

CHICKEN PAPRIKA

Paprika, caraway seeds and soured cream give this dish an Eastern European flavour. Paprika is a seasoning commonly used in Hungary.

SERVES 4

INGREDIENTS:
60 g/2 oz/4 tbsp butter
4 chicken quarters
1 tbsp paprika
1 tbsp caraway seeds
1 onion, chopped finely
1 garlic clove, crushed
1 red (bell) pepper, chopped finely
125 g/4 oz mushrooms, chopped finely
125 g/4 oz pancetta or smoked streaky bacon, diced
75 ml/3 fl oz/¹/₃ cup sherry
150 ml/5 fl oz/²/₃ cup soured cream
1 tbsp cornflour (cornstarch)
salt and pepper

1 Heat the butter in a frying pan (skillet), add the chicken and brown well on all sides. Stir in the paprika and caraway seeds and season. Transfer to an ovenproof dish and set aside.

2 ▼ Add the onion and garlic to the frying pan (skillet) and soften in the butter for about 10 minutes.

3 Add the onion mixture to the chicken. Cover and bake in a preheated oven, 200°C/400°F/Gas Mark 6, for 40 minutes, turning once or twice. Remove the chicken and onions from the dish, reserving the cooking juices. Set aside and keep warm.

4 ▼ Pour the cooking juices into a large frying pan (skillet) set over a moderate heat. Stir in the (bell) pepper, mushrooms and pancetta or bacon, and fry gently for about 15 minutes.

5 ▼ Add the sherry to the pan, and simmer to reduce. Season to taste with salt and pepper.

6 To finish the sauce, combine the soured cream and cornflour (cornstarch) and stir into the pan until the sauce is smooth and thick. Adjust the seasoning and serve with the chicken pieces.

CHICKEN & ALMOND RISSOLES WITH STIR-FRIED VEGETABLES

Cooked potatoes and cooked chicken are combined to make tasty rissoles rolled in chopped almonds to serve with stir-fried vegetables.

SERVES 1

INGREDIENTS:

125 g/4 oz boiled potatoes
90 g/3 oz carrots
125 g/4 oz/1 cup cooked chicken meat
1 garlic clove, crushed
¹/₂ tsp dried tarragon or thyme
generous pinch of ground allspice or ground coriander seeds
1 egg yolk or ¹/₂ egg, beaten
about 30 g/1 oz/¹/₄ cup flaked (slivered) almonds, chopped finely
salt and pepper

STIR-FRIED VEGETABLES:

1 celery stalk
2 spring onions (scallions), trimmed
1 tbsp oil
8 baby sweetcorn cobs
about 10–12 mangetout (snow peas) or sugar snap peas, trimmed
2 tsp balsamic vinegar
salt and pepper

1 ▼ Grate the boiled potatoes and raw carrots coarsely into a bowl. Chop finely or mince (grind) the chicken and add to the vegetables with the garlic, tarragon or thyme, allspice or coriander and salt and pepper.

2 Add the egg yolk or beaten egg and bind the ingredients together. Divide the mixture in half and shape into two sausages.

3 ▼ Roll each rissole in the chopped almonds until evenly coated.

4 Place the rissoles in a greased oven-proof dish and cook in a preheated oven, 200°C/400°F/Gas Mark 6, for about 20 minutes or until lightly browned. Alternatively, fry in a little oil until browned all over and cooked through.

5 ▲ While the rissoles cook, prepare the stir-fried vegetables. Cut the celery and spring onions (scallions) into narrow slanting slices. Heat the oil in a frying pan (skillet) and toss in the vegetables. Cook over a high heat for 1–2 minutes, then add the sweetcorn cobs and mangetout (snowpeas), and cook for 2–3 minutes. Finally, add the balsamic vinegar and season with salt and pepper to taste.

6 Spoon the stir-fried vegetables on to a serving plate and place the rissoles beside them. Serve at once.

CHICKEN, CORIANDER (CILANTRO), GINGER & LEMON STIR-FRY

The pomegranate seeds add a pleasingly sharp Chinese flavour to this Indian stir-fry. The dish can be served cold in the summer with a spicy rice salad or a mixed green salad.

SERVES 4

INGREDIENTS:

3 tbsp oil
750 g/1½ lb skinless, boneless chicken breasts, cut into 5 cm/2 inch strips
3 garlic cloves, crushed
3.5 cm/1½ inch piece fresh ginger root, cut into strips
1 tsp pomegranate seeds, crushed
½ tsp ground turmeric
1 tsp garam masala
2 fresh green chillies, sliced
½ tsp salt
4 tbsp lemon juice
grated rind of 1 lemon
6 tbsp chopped fresh coriander (cilantro)
120 ml/4 fl oz/½ cup chicken stock
naan bread, to serve

1 ▼ Heat the oil in a wok or large frying pan (skillet) and stir-fry the chicken until golden brown all over. Remove from the pan and set aside.

2 Add the garlic, ginger and pomegranate seeds to the pan and fry in the oil for 1 minute taking care not to let the garlic burn.

3 ▼ Stir in the turmeric, garam masala and chillies, and fry for 30 seconds.

4 Return the chicken to the pan and add the salt, lemon juice, lemon rind, coriander (cilantro) and stock. Stir the chicken well to make sure it is coated in the sauce.

5 Bring the mixture to the boil, then lower the heat and simmer for 10–15 minutes until the chicken is thoroughly cooked. Serve with warm naan bread.

CHICKEN WITH PEANUT SAUCE

A tangy stir-fry with a strong peanut flavour. Serve with freshly boiled rice or noodles.

SERVES 4

INGREDIENTS:
4 skinless, boneless chicken breasts
4 tbsp soy sauce
4 tbsp sherry
3 tbsp crunchy peanut butter
350 g/12 oz courgettes (zucchini), trimmed
2 tbsp sunflower oil
4–6 spring onions (scallions), sliced thinly diagonally
250 g/8 oz can of bamboo shoots, well drained and sliced
salt and pepper
4 tbsp desiccated (shredded) coconut, toasted, to garnish

1 Cut the chicken into thin strips across the grain and season lightly with salt and pepper.

2 Put the soy sauce in a bowl with the sherry and peanut butter, and stir until smooth and well blended.

3 ▲ Cut the courgettes (zucchini) into 5 cm/2 inch lengths and then cut into sticks about 5 mm/¼ inch thick.

4 ▲ Heat the oil in the wok, swirling it around until it is really hot. Add the spring onions (scallions) and stir-fry for 1–2 minutes, then add the chicken and stir-fry for 3–4 minutes until well sealed and almost cooked.

5 Add the courgettes (zucchini) and bamboo shoots and continue to stir-fry for 1–2 minutes.

6 ▼ Add the peanut butter mixture and heat thoroughly, stirring all the time so everything is coated in the sauce as it thickens. Adjust the seasoning and serve very hot, sprinkled with the toasted coconut.

CHICKEN WITH MUSHROOMS

If possible, use dried Chinese mushrooms (shiitake) for this dish.

SERVES 4

INGREDIENTS:
300–350 g/10–12 oz skinless, boneless chicken thighs
1/2 tsp sugar
1 tbsp light soy sauce
1 tsp rice wine or dry sherry
2 tsp cornflour (cornstarch)
4–6 dried Chinese mushrooms, soaked in warm water and drained
1 tbsp finely shredded fresh ginger root
a few drops of sesame oil
salt and pepper
coriander (cilantro) leaves, to garnish

1 ▼ Cut the chicken into small bite-sized pieces and place in a bowl. Add the sugar, soy sauce, wine and cornflour (cornstarch) and leave to marinate for 25–30 minutes.

2 ▼ Dry the mushrooms on paper towels. Slice into thin shreds, discarding any hard pieces of stem.

3 ▲ Place the chicken pieces on a heat-proof dish that will fit inside a bamboo steamer. Arrange the mushroom and ginger shreds on top of the chicken and sprinkle with sesame oil, and salt and pepper.

4 ▼ Place the dish on the rack inside a hot steamer or on a rack in a wok or large frying pan (skillet) filled with hot water and steam over high heat for 20 minutes. Serve hot, garnished with coriander (cilantro) leaves.

CHICKEN WITH (BELL) PEPPER

Red (bell) pepper or celery can also be used in this spicy Szechuan recipe, the method is the same.

SERVES 4

INGREDIENTS:
300 g/10 oz skinless, boneless chicken breasts
1 tsp salt
¹/₂ egg white
1 tsp cornflour (cornstarch) mixed to a paste with 1¹/₂ tsp cold water
1 green (bell) pepper, deseeded
300 ml/¹/₂ pint/1¹/₄ cups vegetable oil
1 spring onion (scallion), shredded finely
a few strips of fresh ginger root, shredded thinly
1–2 red chillies, deseeded and shredded thinly
¹/₂ tsp sugar
1 tbsp rice wine or dry sherry
a few drops of sesame oil

1 ▼ Cut the chicken breast into strips, then mix in a bowl with a pinch of the salt, the egg white and cornflour (cornstarch) paste, in that order.

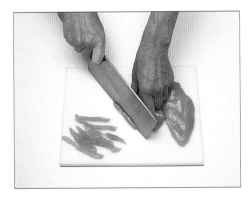

2 Cut the (bell) pepper into thin shreds the same size and length as the chicken strips. Set aside.

3 ▲ Heat the vegetable oil in a preheated wok or frying pan (skillet) to 180–190°C/350–375°F or until a cube of bread browns in 30 seconds. Deep-fry the chicken strips in batches for about 1 minute or until the colour changes and the strips are sealed. Remove with a perforated spoon, set aside and keep warm.

4 ▼ Pour off the excess oil from the wok, leaving about 1 tablespoon. Add the spring onion (scallion), ginger, chillies and (bell) pepper. Stir-fry for about 1 minute, then return the chicken to the wok together with the remaining salt, the sugar and wine or sherry. Stir-fry for 1 minute, sprinkle with sesame oil and serve.

CHICKEN WITH CELERY & CASHEW NUTS

Yellow bean sauce gives this easy dish an authentic Chinese taste. Pecan nuts can be used in place of the cashews.

SERVES 4

INGREDIENTS:
3–4 skinless, boneless chicken breasts, about 625 g/1¼ lb
2 tbsp sunflower or vegetable oil
125 g/4 oz/1 cup unsalted cashew nuts
4–6 spring onions (scallions), sliced thinly diagonally
5–6 celery stalks, sliced thinly diagonally
175 g/6 oz bottle of stir-fry yellow bean sauce
salt and pepper
boiled rice, to serve
celery leaves, to garnish (optional)

1 ▼ Cut the chicken into thin slices across the grain.

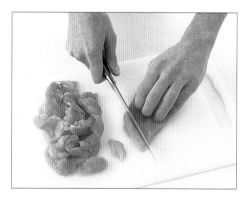

2 ▼ Heat the oil in the wok, swirling it around until hot. Add the cashew nuts and stir-fry until they begin to brown, then add the chicken and stir-fry until well sealed and almost cooked through.

3 ▲ Add the spring onions (scallions) and celery and continue to stir-fry for 2–3 minutes, stirring the ingredients well around the wok.

4 ▲ Stir in the yellow bean sauce, season lightly with salt and pepper and toss until the chicken and vegetables are thoroughly coated with the sauce and are piping hot. Serve at once with plain boiled rice, garnished with celery leaves, if liked.

QUICK CHINESE CHICKEN WITH NOODLES

Chicken and fresh vegetables are flavoured with ginger and Chinese five-spice powder in this quick and easy stir-fry. Vary your choice of vegetables according to what is in season. Make sure that the vegetables are as fresh as possible.

SERVES 4

INGREDIENTS:
175 g/6 oz Chinese thread egg noodles
2 tbsp vegetable oil
30 g/1 oz/¼ cup peanuts
1 bunch of spring onions (scallions), sliced
1 green (bell) pepper, deseeded and cut into thin strips
1 large carrot, cut into matchstick strips
125 g/4 oz cauliflower, broken into small florets
350 g/12 oz skinless, boneless chicken, cut into strips
250 g/8 oz mushrooms, sliced
1 tsp finely grated fresh ginger root
1 tsp Chinese five-spice powder
1 tbsp chopped fresh coriander (cilantro)
1 tbsp light soy sauce
salt and pepper
fresh chives, to garnish

1 Put the noodles into a large bowl and cover with boiling water. Leave to soak for 6 minutes, or according to the instructions on the packet.

2 ▲ Meanwhile, heat the vegetable oil in a preheated wok or large frying pan (skillet). Add the peanuts and stir-fry

for about 1 minute until browned. Remove with a perforated spoon and drain on paper towels.

3 ▲ Add the spring onions (scallions), (bell) pepper, carrot, cauliflower and chicken strips to the pan. Stir-fry over a high heat for 4–5 minutes, until the chicken is cooked thoroughly. The vegetables should remain crisp and brightly coloured.

4 ▼ Drain the noodles thoroughly and add them to the wok. Add the mushrooms and stir-fry for 2 minutes. Add the ginger, five-spice powder and coriander (cilantro) and stir-fry for 1 more minute.

5 Season with the soy sauce, and salt and pepper. Sprinkle with the peanuts, garnish with chives and serve at once on warmed plates.

LIME & CORIANDER (CILANTRO) CHICKEN FRIED RICE

Lime rind and juice is combined with chopped fresh coriander (cilantro) to give this dish a very lively Thai flavour.

SERVES 4

INGREDIENTS:

250 g/8 oz/generous 1 cup long-grain white rice
4 tbsp vegetable oil
2 garlic cloves, chopped finely
1 small green chilli, deseeded and chopped finely
5 shallots, sliced finely
1 tbsp Thai green curry paste
1 yellow or green (bell) pepper, deseeded and chopped
2 celery stalks, sliced finely
250 g/8 oz/1½ cups cooked skinless, boneless chicken, chopped
2 tbsp light soy sauce
finely grated rind of 1 lime
2 tbsp lime juice
1 tbsp chopped fresh coriander (cilantro)
30 g/1 oz/¼ cup unsalted peanuts, toasted

TO GARNISH:
sprigs of fresh coriander (cilantro)
finely sliced shallots
lime slices

1 Cook the rice in plenty of boiling, lightly salted water until tender, about 12 minutes. Drain, rinse with cold water and drain thoroughly.

2 ▲ Heat the oil in a wok or large frying pan (skillet) and add the garlic.

Fry gently for 2 minutes until golden. Add the chilli and shallots, and cook, stirring, for a further 3–4 minutes until slightly softened.

3 ▲ Add the curry paste to the wok and fry for 1 minute, then add the (bell) pepper and the celery. Stir-fry briskly over high heat for 2 minutes until just softened.

4 ▲ Tip the cooked rice into the wok, stirring well, then add the chicken, soy sauce, lime rind and juice, and coriander (cilantro). Stir-fry over a medium-high heat for 4–5 minutes, until the rice and chicken are heated.

5 Serve sprinkled with the peanuts and garnished with sprigs of fresh coriander (cilantro), sliced shallots and lime slices.

GRILLS & ROASTS

There is nothing more delicious than the juicy flesh and slightly charred skin of a piece of chicken grilled (broiled) over an open fire. Lightly brushed with olive oil and seasoned with coarsely ground black pepper, grilled (broiled) chicken is simplicity itself. Marinating the chicken beforehand adds to the flavour and helps prevent it from drying out. Try an Indian-style mixture of yogurt and fragrant spices, or soy sauce, sesame and ginger for an Asian flavour, or try the Cajun-inspired marinade in Blackened Chicken with Guacamole. Roasting is another time-honoured way of cooking chicken. Golden and glistening, traditional roast chicken turns the simplest meal into a celebration.

CHICKEN SATAY KEBABS (PAGE 73)

STICKY CHICKEN WINGS

These need to be eaten with your fingers so serve them at an informal supper.

SERVES 4-6

INGREDIENTS:
1 small onion, finely chopped
2 garlic cloves, crushed
2 tbsp olive oil
450 ml/³⁄₄ pint tomato passata
2 tsp dried thyme
1 tsp dried oregano
pinch fennel seeds
3 tbsp red wine vinegar
2 tbsp Dijon mustard
pinch ground cinnamon
2 tbsp brown sugar
1 tsp chilli flakes
2 tbsp black treacle
16 chicken wings
salt and pepper

1 ▼ Soften the onion and garlic in the oil for about 10 minutes.

2 ▼ Add the passata, dried herbs, fennel, vinegar, mustard and cinnamon to the pan along with the sugar, chilli

flakes, treacle, and salt and pepper. Bring to the boil, then reduce the heat and simmer gently for about 15 minutes, until slightly reduced.

3 ▲ Put the chicken wings in a large dish, and coat liberally with the sauce. Marinade for 3 hours or as long as possible, stirring often.

4 ▼ Transfer the wings to a clean baking sheet (cookie sheet), and roast in a preheated oven, 220°C/425°F/Gas Mark 7, for 10 minutes. Reduce the heat to 190°C/375°F/Gas Mark 5 and cook for 20 minutes, basting often.

5 Serve piping hot, garnished with celery stalks and cherry tomatoes.

LEMON & MINT CHICKEN BURGERS

Use chicken thigh or leg meat for these delicious burgers – it has much more flavour than breast meat.

SERVES 4

INGREDIENTS:
750 g/1½ lb minced chicken leg meat
4 tbsp chopped fresh mint
grated rind of 1 lemon
4 tbsp lemon juice
olive oil
90 g/3 oz pitted black olives, chopped
salt
lemon pepper (or black pepper)
1 round focaccia bread – either plain or flavoured
lettuce and lemon wedges, to garnish

1 ▼ In a large bowl, combine the chicken, mint, lemon rind, lemon juice, 1 tablespoon of olive oil, black olives, salt and lemon pepper. Leave to marinate for at least 2 hours.

2 ▼ Form the mixture into four patties, pressing between your hands. Chill until ready to serve.

3 ▲ When ready to serve, cut the focaccia into four quarters, halve horizontally and liberally brush each half with olive oil. Toast under a grill (broiler) – do not use a toaster.

4 Brush the burgers on both sides with a little olive oil. Place on a rack under a preheated hot grill (broiler) for about 10 minutes, turning once, until thoroughly cooked through. To serve, place each burger between two pieces of toasted focaccia, and garnish with lettuce and lemon wedges.

BARBECUED CHICKEN

You need a bit of brute force to prepare the chicken, but once marinated it's an easy and tasty candidate for the barbecue.

SERVES 4

INGREDIENTS:
1.5 kg/3 lb chicken
grated rind of 1 lemon
4 tbsp lemon juice
2 sprigs of rosemary
1 small red chilli, deseeded and
*   chopped finely*
150 ml/¹⁄₄ pint/²⁄₃ cup olive oil

TO SERVE:
minted new potatoes
green salad

1 ▼ Split the chicken down the breast bone and open it out, breaking the leg and wing joints to enable you to flatten it.

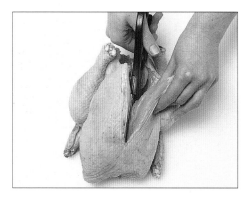

2 ▼ Cover with clingfilm (plastic wrap) and pound flat with a rolling pin. This ensures that it cooks evenly.

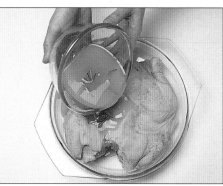

3 ▲ Mix the lemon rind and juice, rosemary sprigs, chilli and olive oil together in a small bowl. Place the chicken in a dish and pour over the marinade, turning the chicken to coat it evenly. Cover the dish and leave the chicken to marinate in the refrigerator for at least 2 hours or overnight. Allow to come to room temperature for 30 minutes before cooking.

4 ▼ Cook the chicken over a hot barbecue (the coals should be white and red when fanned) for about 30 minutes, turning it regularly until the skin is golden and crisp. To test if it is cooked, pierce one of the chicken thighs; if it is ready, the juices should run clear, not pink. Serve with minted new potatoes and a green salad.

CHICKEN IN SPICY YOGURT

This dish is ideal for cooking on a barbecue, but make sure the barbecue is really hot. The coals should be white and glow red when fanned. You could also cook the chicken under a very hot preheated grill (broiler).

SERVES 6

INGREDIENTS:
3 dried red chillies
2 tbsp coriander seed
2 tsp turmeric
2 tsp garam masala
4 garlic cloves, crushed
½ onion, chopped
2.5cm/1 inch piece fresh ginger root, grated
2 tbsp lime juice
1 tsp salt
120 ml/4 fl oz/½ cup natural yogurt
1 tbsp oil
2 kg/4 lb chicken, cut into 6 pieces, or 6 chicken portions

TO SERVE:
chopped tomatoes
diced cucumber
sliced red onion
Cucumber Raita (page 70)

1 Grind together the chillies, coriander, turmeric, garam masala, garlic, onion, ginger, lime juice and salt with a pestle and mortar or grinder.

2 ▼ Heat the spice paste in a frying pan (skillet) over a low heat. Stir for about 2 minutes until fragrant. Turn into a shallow non-porous bowl.

3 ▼ Add the yogurt and oil to the spice paste, and mix well.

4 Remove the skin from the chicken portions and make three slashes in the flesh of each piece. Add the chicken to the dish and make sure that the pieces are coated completely in the marinade. Cover and chill for at least 4 hours. Remove from the refrigerator and leave covered at room temperature for 30 minutes before cooking.

5 Wrap the chicken pieces in foil, sealing well so the juices cannot escape. Cook the chicken pieces over a very hot barbecue for about 15 minutes, turning once.

6 ▼ Remove the foil, with the aid of a pair of tongs, and brown the chicken on the barbecue for 5 minutes. Serve with the chopped tomatoes, diced cucumber, sliced red onion, and the cucumber raita.

CHARGRILLED CHICKEN SALAD

This is a quick dish to serve at a barbecue while your hungry guests are waiting for the main event. If the bread is bent in half, the chicken salad can be put in the middle and eaten as finger food – remember to provide napkins!

SERVES 4

INGREDIENTS:
2 skinless, boneless chicken breasts
1 red onion
oil for brushing
1 avocado, pitted
1 tbsp lemon juice
120 ml/4 fl oz/$\frac{1}{2}$ cup mayonnaise
$\frac{1}{4}$ tsp chilli powder
$\frac{1}{2}$ tsp pepper
$\frac{1}{4}$ tsp salt
4 tomatoes, quartered
1 round sun-dried tomato-flavoured
　focaccia bread
green salad, to serve

1 Cut the chicken breasts into 1 cm/ $\frac{1}{2}$ inch strips.

2 ▲ Cut the onion into eight pieces, held together at the root. Rinse under cold running water, pat dry and then brush with oil.

3 Purée or mash the avocado and lemon juice together. Whisk in the mayonnaise. Add the chilli powder, pepper and salt.

4 ▼ Put the chicken and onion over a hot barbecue, and grill (broil) for 3–4 minutes on each side until beginning to blacken.

5 Combine the blackened chicken and onion with the avocado mixture, then stir in the tomatoes.

6 ▲ Cut the focaccia in half twice, so that you have quarter-circle-shaped pieces, then slice in half horizontally. Toast on the hot barbecue for about 2 minutes on each side.

7 Spoon the chicken mixture over the toasts and serve with a green salad.

MEDITERRANEAN GRILLED CHICKEN

Chargrilling and barbecuing over hot embers is a way of life in the Mediterranean countries. This recipe from the Languedoc area of France, uses crisp, juicy chicken.

SERVES 4

INGREDIENTS:
4 tbsp natural yogurt
3 tbsp sun-dried tomato paste
1 tbsp olive oil
15 g/¹/₂ oz/¹/₄ cup fresh basil leaves,
  lightly crushed
2 garlic cloves, chopped roughly
4 chicken quarters
coarse sea salt
green salad, to serve

1 ▼ Combine the yogurt, tomato paste, olive oil, basil leaves and garlic in a small bowl and stir well to mix.

2 ▼ Put the marinade into a bowl large enough to hold the chicken quarters in a single layer. Add the chicken quarters, making sure they are thoroughly coated in the marinade.

3 Leave the chicken to marinate in the refrigerator for at least 2 hours or overnight. Remove and leave, covered, at room temperature for 30 minutes before cooking.

4 ▼ Place the chicken over a medium-hot barbecue and grill (broil) for 30–40 minutes, turning frequently.

5 ▲ Test for doneness by piercing the flesh at the top of the drumstick. If the juices run clear, the chicken is cooked. If the juices are pink, cook for 10 minutes more.

6 Sprinkle with coarse sea salt and serve hot with a green salad. This dish is also delicious eaten cold.

SPICY CHICKEN TIKKA

To prevent bamboo skewers charring during cooking, soak them first in cold water for 30 minutes before threading with the chicken.

SERVES 6

INGREDIENTS:
500 g/1 lb skinless, boneless chicken breasts
1½ tbsp Tikka paste (from a jar)
6 tbsp thick natural yogurt
1 tbsp lemon juice
½ onion, chopped finely
1½ tbsp chopped chives or spring onion (scallion) tops
1½ tbsp finely chopped fresh ginger root
1–2 garlic cloves, crushed
1½ tbsp sesame seeds
2 tbsp vegetable oil
lemon or lime juice for sprinkling
salt and pepper

1 Cut the chicken breasts into small bite-sized pieces, place in a shallow glass dish, and season with salt and pepper to taste.

2 ▲ In a small bowl, mix together the remaining ingredients, except the sesame seeds, oil and lemon or lime juice, and pour over the chicken. Mix well until all the chicken pieces are coated, then cover and chill for at least 1 hour, or for longer if possible.

3 ▼ Thread the chicken pieces on to six bamboo or metal skewers and sprinkle with the sesame seeds.

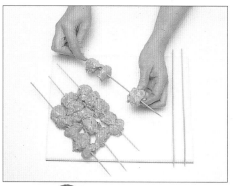

4 ▲ Place on a rack in a grill (broiler) pan and drizzle with the oil. Cook under a hot grill for about 15 minutes or until cooked through and browned, turning frequently and brushing with more oil, if necessary. Serve hot, sprinkled with lemon or lime juice.

CHICKEN TIKKA & MANGO KEBABS

Chicken tikka is one of the lower-fat dishes from India. Recipes vary but you can try your own combination of spices to suit your personal taste.

SERVES 4

INGREDIENTS:
4 × 125 g/4 oz skinless, boneless chicken breasts
1 garlic clove, crushed
1 tsp grated fresh ginger root
1 fresh green chilli, deseeded and chopped finely
6 tbsp low-fat natural yogurt
1 tbsp tomato purée (paste)
1 tsp ground cumin seeds
1 tsp ground coriander seeds
1 tsp ground turmeric
1 large ripe mango
2 tbsp lime juice
salt and pepper

TO GARNISH:
fresh coriander (cilantro) leaves
lime wedges

TO SERVE:
boiled white rice
mixed salad
warmed naan bread

1 Cut the chicken into 2.5 cm/1 inch cubes and place in a shallow dish.

2 ▲ Mix together the garlic, ginger, chilli, yogurt, tomato purée (paste), cumin, coriander, turmeric, and salt and pepper. Spoon over the chicken, mix well, cover and chill for 2 hours.

3 Using a vegetable peeler, peel the skin from the mango. Slice down either side of the stone (pit) and cut the flesh into cubes. Toss in the lime juice, then cover and store in the refrigerator until required.

4 ▼ Thread the chicken and mango pieces on to eight skewers. Place on a grill (broiler) rack and brush the chicken with the yogurt marinade and any remaining lime juice.

5 Place under a preheated moderate grill (broiler) for 6–7 minutes. Turn over, brush again with the yogurt marinade and lime juice and cook for a further 6–7 minutes until the chicken juices run clear when the cubes are pierced with a sharp knife.

6 Serve on a bed of rice on a warmed platter with fresh coriander (cilantro) leaves, lime wedges, a mixed salad and warmed naan bread.

TANDOORI CHICKEN

The tandoor is a traditional Indian oven shaped like a huge urn. Charcoal is burnt slowly at the bottom until it becomes a mass of white-hot coals.

SERVES 4

INGREDIENTS:
8 small chicken portions, skinned
3 dried red chillies
1 tsp salt
2 tsp coriander seeds
2 tbsp lime juice
2 garlic cloves, crushed
2.5 cm/1 inch piece fresh ginger root, grated
1 clove
2 tsp garam masala
2 tsp chilli powder
1/2 onion, chopped
300 ml/1/2 pint/1 1/4 cups natural yogurt
1 tbsp chopped fresh coriander (cilantro)
lemon slices, to garnish

CUCUMBER RAITA:
250 g/8 oz/1 cup natural yogurt
2 tsp chopped fresh mint
175 g/6 oz cucumber, peeled, deseeded and cut into matchstick strips
salt

1 Make 2–3 slashes in the flesh of the chicken pieces with a sharp knife and put in a non-metallic dish.

2 ▼ Crush the chillies, salt, coriander seeds, lime juice, garlic, ginger and clove. Stir in the garam masala and chilli powder. Transfer to a saucepan and heat gently until aromatic.

3 ▼ Remove the pan from the heat. Add the onion and yogurt.

4 Pour the yogurt mixture over the chicken. Cover and leave to marinate in the refrigerator for at least 4 hours or preferably overnight.

5 Combine the raita ingredients in a small bowl. Cover and chill.

6 Arrange the chicken in a grill (broiler) pan and cook under a preheated very hot grill (broiler) or over a barbecue for 20–30 minutes, turning once, until the juices run clear when the thickest parts of the portions are pierced with a sharp knife.

7 Sprinkle the chicken with chopped fresh coriander (cilantro). Serve hot or cold, garnished with the lemon slices and accompanied by cucumber raita.

SESAME SKEWERED CHICKEN WITH GINGER BASTE

Chunks of chicken breast are marinated in a mixture of lime juice, garlic, sesame oil and fresh ginger to give them a great flavour. The kebabs taste even more delicious if dipped into an accompanying bowl of hot chilli sauce.

SERVES 4

INGREDIENTS:
500 g/1 lb boneless chicken breasts
sprigs of fresh mint, to garnish

MARINADE:
1 garlic clove, crushed
1 shallot, chopped very finely
2 tbsp sesame oil
1 tbsp fish sauce or light soy sauce
finely grated rind of 1 lime or ½ lemon
2 tbsp lime juice or lemon juice
1 tsp sesame seeds
2 tsp finely grated fresh ginger root
2 tsp chopped fresh mint
salt and pepper

1 ▼ To make the marinade, put the garlic, shallot, sesame oil, fish sauce or soy sauce, lime or lemon rind and juice, sesame seeds, ginger and chopped mint into a large non-metallic bowl. Season to taste with a little salt and pepper.

2 ▼ Remove the skin from the chicken breasts and cut the flesh into chunks. Add the chicken chunks to the marinade, stirring to coat them in the mixture. Cover and chill in the refrigerator for at least 2 hours, preferably longer. Soak 12 wooden skewers in warm water for 30 minutes. This will prevent them scorching during cooking.

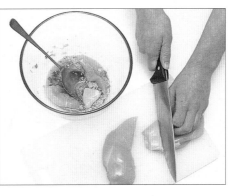

3 ▼ Thread the chicken on to the skewers. Place them in a foil-lined grill (broiler) pan and liberally baste with the marinade.

4 Place the kebabs under a preheated grill (broiler) for about 8–10 minutes. Turn them frequently, basting with the remaining marinade. Serve at once, garnished with sprigs of fresh mint.

CRISPY CHICKEN DRUMSTICKS

Just the thing to put on the barbecue – chicken drumsticks, coated with a spicy, curry-like butter, then grilled until crispy and golden. Serve with a green seasonal salad and rice.

SERVES 6

INGREDIENTS:
12 chicken drumsticks

SPICED BUTTER:
175 g/6 oz/³⁄₄ cup butter
2 garlic cloves, crushed
1 tsp grated fresh ginger root
2 tsp ground turmeric
4 tsp cayenne pepper
2 tbsp lime juice
3 tbsp mango chutney

TO SERVE:
green salad
boiled rice

1 Prepare a barbecue with medium coals or preheat a conventional grill (broiler) to moderate.

2 ▲ To make the spiced butter mixture, beat the butter with the garlic, ginger, turmeric, cayenne pepper, lime juice and chutney until it is blended well.

3 ▼ Using a sharp knife, slash each chicken drumstick to the bone 3–4 times. Place on a rack under a preheated hot grill (broiler) and cook for 12–15 minutes until almost cooked, turning halfway through. Alternatively, cook them over the barbecue for about 12–15 minutes.

4 ▲ Spread the chicken legs liberally with the butter mixture and continue to cook for a further 5–6 minutes, turning and basting frequently with the butter until golden and crisp.

5 Serve hot or cold with a crisp green salad and rice.

CHICKEN SATAY KEBABS

Small kebabs of satay chicken with cubes of cheese and cherry tomatoes are served on crisp lettuce leaves. These are ideal for a starter or to take on a picnic.

MAKES 8

INGREDIENTS:

1 tbsp sherry
1 tbsp light soy sauce
1 tbsp sesame oil
finely grated rind of ¹/₂ lemon
1 tbsp lemon or lime juice
2 tsp sesame seeds
500 g/1 lb skinless, boneless chicken breasts
90 g/3 oz Double Gloucester (brick) cheese or Gouda cheese
16 cherry tomatoes
crisp lettuce leaves, such as Little Gem
salt and pepper

PEANUT DIP:

30 g/1 oz/¹/₃ cup desiccated (shredded) coconut
150 ml/¹/₄ pint/²/₃ cup boiling water
125 g/4 oz/¹/₂ cup crunchy peanut butter
good pinch of chilli powder
1 tsp brown sugar
1 tbsp light soy sauce
2 spring onions (scallions), trimmed and chopped

1 In a bowl, combine the sherry, soy sauce, sesame oil, lemon rind, lemon or lime juice, sesame seeds, and salt and pepper.

2 Cut the chicken into 2.5 cm/1 inch cubes. Add to the marinade and mix well. Cover and leave to chill in the refrigerator for 3–6 hours.

3 To make the dip, put the coconut in a saucepan with the boiling water and bring back to the boil. Set aside until cold. Add the peanut butter, chilli powder, sugar and soy sauce and bring slowly to the boil. Simmer very gently, stirring all the time, for 2–3 minutes until thickened, then leave to cool. Meanwhile, soak eight wooden skewers in warm water for 30 minutes.

4 ▲ Stir the spring onions (scallions) into the peanut mixture and turn into a serving bowl.

5 Thread the chicken on to the skewers, positioning them in the centre. Cook under a preheated moderate grill (broiler) for about 5 minutes on each side until cooked through. Leave until cold.

6 ▼ Cut the cheese into 16 cubes and then thread one of these and a cherry tomato on to each end of the skewers.

7 To serve, arrange each kebab on a crisp lettuce leaf and serve with the peanut dip.

BLACKENED CHICKEN WITH GUACAMOLE

This easy recipe is typical of French Cajun cooking which has its roots in earthy, strong flavours, and uses plenty of spices. The dish includes a typical Cajun spice mix.

SERVES 4

INGREDIENTS:
4 skinless, boneless chicken breasts
60 g/2 oz/¹/₄ cup butter, melted

CAJUN SPICE MIXTURE:
1 tsp salt
1 tbsp sweet paprika
1 tsp dried onion granules
1 tsp dried garlic granules
1 tsp dried thyme
1 tsp cayenne
¹/₂ tsp cracked black pepper
¹/₂ tsp dried oregano

GUACAMOLE:
1 avocado
1 tbsp lemon juice
2 tbsp soured cream
¹/₂ red onion, chopped
1 garlic clove, halved

1 Put the chicken breasts between two pieces of clingfilm (plastic wrap), and pound with a mallet or rolling pin to an even thickness. They should be about 1 cm/¹/₂ inch thick.

2 ▼ Brush each chicken breast all over with the melted butter, then set aside.

3 Combine the spice mix ingredients in a shallow bowl.

4 ▲ Dip the chicken breasts in the spice mix, ensuring that they are completely coated. Set aside.

5 To make the guacamole, mash the avocado thoroughly with the lemon juice in a small bowl. Stir in the soured cream and red onion.

6 ▼ Wipe the garlic clove around the guacamole serving dish, pressing hard. Spoon in the guacamole.

7 Place the chicken breasts over the hottest part of a very hot barbecue and cook for 8–10 minutes, turning once.

8 Slice the breasts into thick pieces and serve immediately accompanied by the guacamole.

JERK CHICKEN

This is a popular Caribbean dish. Rubbing pastes and 'rubs' into meat, poultry or seafood is a technique first introduced by the Arawak Indians, and helps to tenderize the meat.

SERVES 6

INGREDIENTS:
1.5 kg/3 lb chicken pieces
cherry tomatoes, to garnish
salad, to serve

MARINADE:
6 spring onions (scallions)
2 fresh red chillies, preferably Scotch bonnet
2 tbsp dark soy sauce
2 tbsp lime juice
3 tsp ground allspice
1/2 tsp ground bay leaves
1 tsp ground cinnamon
2 garlic cloves, chopped
2 tsp brown sugar
1 tsp dried thyme
1/2 tsp salt

1 ▼ To make the marinade, chop the spring onions (scallions). Deseed and chop the chillies.

2 Put the spring onions (scallions), chillies and the remaining marinade ingredients into a food processor and blend until smooth. Alternatively, chop the spring onions (scallions) and chillies very finely (being careful not to touch your eyes), add these to the remaining ingredients and, using a pestle and mortar, work to a chunky paste.

3 ▼ Place the chicken pieces in a shallow dish and generously spoon over the marinade. Cover and put into the refrigerator to marinate for 24 hours, turning each piece of chicken several times to make sure it is evenly marinated.

4 ▲ Brush a grill (broiler) rack with oil and place the chicken on top. Grill (broil) under a preheated medium grill (broiler) for about 15–20 minutes on each side until the chicken juices run clear when the thickest part of the flesh is pierced with a sharp knife.

FILIPINO CHICKEN

Tomato ketchup is used in this recipe from the Philippines. It is a very popular ingredient as it has a zingy sweet-sour flavour.

SERVES 4

INGREDIENTS:
1 can lemonade or lime-and-lemonade
2 tbsp gin
4 tbsp tomato ketchup
2 tsp garlic salt
2 tsp Worcestershire sauce
4 chicken supremes or breasts
salt and pepper

TO SERVE:
thread egg noodles
1 green chilli, chopped finely
2 spring onions (scallions), sliced

1 ▼ Combine the lemonade or lime-and-lemonade, gin, tomato ketchup, garlic salt, Worcestershire sauce and seasoning in a large non-porous dish.

2 ▼ Put the chicken pieces into the dish, ensuring they are covered.

3 Cover and leave to marinate in the refrigerator for 2 hours. Remove and allow to come to room temperature for 30 minutes before cooking.

4 ▲ Place the chicken over a medium-hot barbecue and cook for 20 minutes, turning once, until completely cooked through.

5 Remove the chicken from the barbecue and leave to rest for 3–4 minutes.

6 Carve into thin slices and serve with egg noodles, tossed with a little green chilli and spring onions (scallions).

THAI CHICKEN WITH PEANUT SAUCE

This is a favourite Thai dish served with a spicy peanut sauce. It can be made with chicken or beef.

SERVES 4–6

INGREDIENTS:
4 skinless, boneless chicken breasts

MARINADE:
1 small onion, finely chopped
1 garlic clove, crushed
2.5 cm/1 inch piece fresh ginger root, grated
2 tbsp dark soy sauce
2 tsp chilli powder
1 tsp ground coriander seeds
2 tsp dark brown sugar
1 tbsp lemon or lime juice
1 tbsp vegetable oil

SPICY PEANUT SAUCE:
300 ml/¹/₂ pint/1¹/₄ cups coconut milk
4 tbsp/¹/₃ cup crunchy peanut butter
1 tbsp fish sauce
1 tsp lemon or lime juice
salt and pepper

1 Trim any fat from the chicken breasts then cut into thin strips, about 7 cm/3 inches long.

2 ▼ To make the marinade, place all the ingredients in a shallow dish and mix well. Add the chicken strips and turn in the marinade until well coated. Cover and put in the refrigerator to marinate for at least 2 hours or overnight. Meanwhile, soak six wooden skewers for 30 minutes.

3 ▼ Remove the chicken from the marinade and thread the pieces, concertina style, on to the skewers.

4 Grill (broil) the chicken for 8–10 minutes, turning and brushing occasionally with the marinade, until cooked.

5 ▼ Meanwhile, to make the spicy peanut sauce, mix the coconut milk with the peanut butter, fish sauce and lemon or lime juice in a saucepan. Bring to the boil and cook for 3 minutes. Season with salt and pepper to taste. Pour into a serving bowl and serve with the chicken.

CRISPY-COATED BABY CHICKENS

You could adapt this recipe using a whole chicken or chicken pieces, serving them on a bed of moist and colourful vegetables.

SERVES 6

INGREDIENTS:
4 tbsp vegetable oil
60 g/2 oz/¼ cup butter
6 small baby chickens, trussed
1 large onion, sliced
500 g/1 lb baby carrots
1 tbsp flour
150 ml/¼ pint/⅔ cup white wine
juice of 2 oranges
2 fennel bulbs, quartered
300 ml/½ pint/1¼ cups chicken stock
½ tsp salt
1 tbsp black peppercorns, lightly crushed
1 tsp cornflour (cornstarch)
150 ml/¼ pint/⅔ cup thick natural yogurt
salt and pepper

COATING:
3 tbsp demerara (brown crystal) sugar
1 tbsp black peppercorns, lightly crushed
3 tbsp coarse sea salt
150 ml/¼ pint/⅔ cup thick natural yogurt

1 ▼ Heat the oil in a large heavy-based frying pan (skillet) and add the butter. When bubbling, add the baby chickens in batches and brown evenly on all sides. Remove from the pan and keep warm.

2 Add the onion to the pan and fry until translucent. Add the carrots, stir to coat evenly, then sprinkle on the flour and blend well. Pour on the wine and orange juice, stirring all the time. Add the fennel, chicken stock, salt and peppercorns. Bring to the boil then pour into a large roasting tin (pan).

3 ▲ Arrange the baby chickens in the roasting tin (pan), cover with foil and cook in a preheated oven, 180°C/350°F/Gas Mark 4, for 40 minutes.

4 To make the coating, stir together the sugar, peppercorns, salt and yogurt to make a thick paste.

5 ▼ Remove the chickens from the roasting tin (pan) and place them on a rack in a grill pan. Spread the paste evenly over the chickens then grill (broil) under a hot preheated grill (broiler) for 3–4 minutes, until crisp.

6 Remove the vegetables in the tin (pan) with a perforated spoon and place on a warm serving dish. Place the tin (pan) over medium heat and bring the pan juices to the boil. Stir the cornflour (cornstarch) into the yogurt then blend into the juices. Check the seasoning. Place the chickens on the serving dish, spoon over a little sauce, and serve the rest separately.

BABY CHICKENS WITH GREEN PEPPERCORNS

Baby chickens are a great alternative to ordinary chicken. One bird serves two people and can be cooked whole.

SERVES 4

INGREDIENTS:
2 baby chickens, halved lengthways
2 tbsp oil
30 g/1 oz/2 tbsp butter
1 onion, chopped
3 tbsp bottled green peppercorns
2 tbsp coarse-grain mustard
120 ml/4 fl oz/½ cup white wine
200 g/7 oz/1 cup basmati and wild rice
500 ml/16 fl oz/2 cups chicken stock
salt and pepper
sautéd cherry tomatoes, to serve
sprigs of fresh thyme, to garnish

1 ▽ Wash the chicken halves and pat dry. Season well with salt and pepper.

2 ▽ Heat the oil and butter in a frying pan (skillet). Fry the onions gently for 5 minutes until soft. Add the chickens and fry until evenly browned.

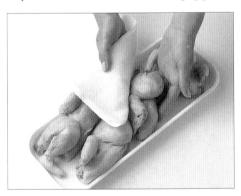

3 Transfer the chickens to a roasting tin (pan). Roast in a preheated oven, 200°C/400°F/Gas Mark 6, for about 30 minutes.

4 ▲ Meanwhile, stir the peppercorns, mustard and wine into the juices in the frying pan. Bring to the boil and reduce by half.

5 ▽ Stir in the rice, and pour on the stock. Season well and bring to the boil. Reduce the heat and simmer for 18–20 minutes. Adjust the seasoning, if necessary.

6 Serve the chickens with rice accompanied by sautéd tomatoes. Garnish with a sprig of thyme.

TRADITIONAL ROAST CHICKEN

Roast chicken is an all-time classic which pleases everyone.

SERVES 4–6

INGREDIENTS:
4 slices streaky bacon
8 chipolata sausages
1 roasting chicken, about 2 kg/4 lb,
    with giblets
60 g/2 oz/4 tbsp butter
1 kg/2 lb potatoes
watercress, to garnish

STUFFING:
60 g/2 oz white crustless bread
125 g/4 oz minced pork sausagemeat
1 tbsp chopped mixed fresh herbs
1 tbsp chopped fresh sage
chicken livers from the giblets, washed
    and dried

BREAD SAUCE:
300 ml/1/2 pint/1 1/4 cups milk
90 g/3 oz crustless white bread
1 onion pierced with 10 cloves
30 g/1 oz/2 tbsp butter
pinch ground allspice
1 tbsp double (heavy) cream
1 tbsp plain (all-purpose) flour
150 ml/1/4 pint/2/3 cup chicken stock
2–3 tbsp sherry

1 ▼ Cut the bacon in half widthways, and stretch with the back of a knife. Wrap each piece around a chipolata sausage and set aside.

2 Wash and dry the breast cavity of the chicken.

3 To make the stuffing, turn on the food processor, and insert the bread through the feed tube. Process until finely crumbed. Now add the sausagemeat, mixed herbs, sage, and the chicken livers. Alternatively, grate the bread to form crumbs, chop the livers, and mash together with the other stuffing ingredients.

4 Spoon the stuffing in through the neck end of the bird, using the loose skin to make a pocket of stuffing, filling out the breast.

5 ▲ Fasten the flap of skin underneath neatly, with string or skewers. Put any remaining stuffing in the cavity at the other end.

6 Transfer the chicken to a roasting tin (pan), and pat the butter all over. Cover loosely with parchment and bake in a preheated oven, 200°C/400°F/Gas Mark 6, for 20 minutes.

7 Meanwhile, cut the potatoes to an even size. Parboil in salted boiling water, then drain. Spoon in the potatoes around the chicken, turning to coat in the fat.

8 Reduce the heat to 180°C/350°F/Gas Mark 4 for 1 hour and 20 minutes, basting the chicken at least three times. Add the chipolatas 30 minutes before the end of cooking and remove the parchment 15 minutes before the end. Transfer the potatoes to a serving dish when they are browned and crisp.

9 Meanwhile, to make the bread sauce, put all the ingredients in a saucepan and simmer for 30 minutes. Discard the onion. Set aside and keep warm.

10 Remove the chicken from the oven, leave to rest in a warm place for 20 minutes while you make the gravy. Arrange the potatoes and chipolatas around the chicken, and garnish with watercress. Serve with the bread sauce.

CASSEROLES

Braising or casseroling is one of the classic methods of cooking chicken, producing the most delectable results. The chicken is enclosed in a sealed casserole with aromatic vegetables and herbs, and a small amount of liquid. Cooked at a gentle simmer over the lowest possible heat, or in a low oven, chicken becomes meltingly tender, moistened by enriched juices. One of the most celebrated classic casseroles is the French Coq au Vin, here made with white wine instead of red. Other lip-smacking favourites include Chicken with 40 Garlic Cloves from France, Baton Rouge Gumbo Chicken from New Orleans and Chicken Cacciatora from Italy.

ROMAN CHICKEN (PAGE 87)

CHICKEN CACCIATORA

This is a popular Italian classic in which browned chicken quarters are cooked in a tomato and pepper sauce.

SERVES 4

INGREDIENTS:

1 roasting chicken, about 1.5 kg/ 3 lb,
cut into 6 or 8 serving pieces
125 g/4 oz/1 cup plain (all-purpose) flour
3 tbsp olive oil
150 ml/¼ pint/⅔ cup dry white wine
1 green (bell) pepper, deseeded and sliced
1 red (bell) pepper, deseeded and sliced
1 carrot, chopped finely
1 celery stalk, chopped finely
1 garlic clove, crushed
200 g/7 oz can of chopped tomatoes
salt and pepper

1 ▼ Rinse and pat dry the chicken pieces with paper towels. Lightly dust them with seasoned flour.

2 ▼ Heat the oil in a large frying pan (skillet). Add the chicken and fry over a medium heat until browned all over. Remove from the pan and set aside.

3 ▼ Drain off all but 2 tablespoons of the fat in the pan. Add the wine and stir for a few minutes. Then add the peppers, carrots, celery and garlic, season well and simmer together for about 15 minutes.

4 ▼ Add the chopped tomatoes to the pan. Cover and simmer for 30 minutes, stirring often, until the chicken is cooked through.

5 Check the seasoning before serving piping hot.

CHICKEN WITH 40 GARLIC CLOVES

In France, the chicken is served accompanied by slices of bread. Each diner spreads the bread with the softened and sweetened garlic.

SERVES 4

INGREDIENTS:
*1 roasting chicken, weighing about
 1.5 kg/ 3 lb
15 g/¹/₂ oz fresh thyme
15 g/¹/₂ oz fresh rosemary
15 g/¹/₂ oz fresh sage
15 g/¹/₂ oz fresh parsley
2 small celery stalks
40 fresh garlic cloves, unpeeled
4 tbsp olive oil
salt*

3 ⏶ Place the chicken in a roasting tin (pan) or earthenware dish with the rest of the herbs, celery and garlic. Brush the olive oil all over the skin.

4 Roast in a preheated oven, 200°C/400°F/Gas Mark 6, for 1¹/₂ hours, basting frequently.

5 Transfer the cooked chicken to a warmed serving platter, and surround with the cloves of garlic. Skim most of the fat from the cooking juices. Bring to the boil, and reduce slightly. Strain into a warmed sauce boat to serve.

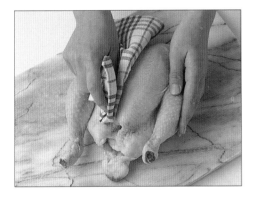

1 ⏶ Wash and pat the chicken dry, rubbing salt into the skin.

2 ▽ Stuff the cavity with half of the fresh herbs, one celery stalk and ten of the garlic cloves.

CHICKEN & BLACK-EYE BEANS (PEAS)

In India and Pakistan, pulses are a valuable source of nourishment in mountainous areas in winter when meat is scarce. You could use any variety of pulses, but you may need to adjust the cooking times accordingly.

SERVES 4

INGREDIENTS:

250 g/8 oz/1 generous cup dried black-eye beans (peas), soaked overnight and drained
1 tsp salt
2 onions, chopped
2 garlic cloves, crushed
1 tsp ground turmeric
1 tsp ground cumin
1.25 kg/2½ lb chicken, jointed into 8 pieces
1 green (bell) pepper, deseeded and chopped
2 tbsp oil
2.5 cm/1 inch piece fresh ginger root, grated
2 tsp coriander seeds
½ tsp fennel seeds
2 tsp garam masala
1 tbsp chopped fresh coriander (cilantro), to garnish

1 ▼ Put the drained beans (peas) into a wok or large frying pan (skillet) with the salt, onions, garlic, turmeric and cumin. Cover with water, bring to the boil and cook for 15 minutes.

2 Add the chicken and (bell) pepper to the wok and bring to the boil. Lower the heat and simmer for 30 minutes until the juices run clear when the thickest parts of the chicken pieces are pierced with a sharp knife.

3 ▼ Heat the oil in a clean wok and fry the ginger, coriander seeds and fennel seeds for 30 seconds.

4 ▼ Stir the ginger, coriander seeds and fennel seeds into the chicken and add the garam masala. Simmer for a further 5 minutes and serve garnished with fresh coriander (cilantro).

CHICKEN & CHILLI BEAN POT

This aromatic Mexican chicken dish has a spicy kick. Chicken thighs are not only more economical than breasts, they have much more flavour when cooked in this way.

SERVES 4

INGREDIENTS:

2 tbsp plain (all-purpose) flour
1 tsp chilli powder
8 chicken thighs or 4 chicken legs
3 tbsp olive or vegetable oil
2 garlic cloves, crushed
1 large onion, chopped
1 green or red (bell) pepper, deseeded and chopped
300 ml/½ pint/1¼ cups chicken stock
350 g/12 oz tomatoes, chopped
425 g/14 oz can of red kidney beans, rinsed and drained
2 tbsp tomato purée (paste)
salt and pepper

1 ▼ Mix together the flour, chilli powder, and salt and pepper in a shallow dish. Rinse the chicken, but do not dry. Dip the chicken into the seasoned flour, coating it on all sides.

2 ▲ Heat the oil in a large, deep frying pan (skillet) or saucepan and add the chicken. Cook over a high heat for 3–4 minutes, turning the pieces to brown them all over. Remove with a perforated spoon and drain on paper towels.

3 Add the garlic, onion and (bell) pepper to the pan and fry gently for 2–3 minutes until softened.

4 ▼ Add the stock, tomatoes, kidney beans and tomato purée (paste), stirring well. Bring to the boil.

5 Return the chicken to the pan. Reduce the heat and simmer, covered, for about 30 minutes, until the chicken is tender. Season with salt and pepper to taste. Transfer to a warm serving dish and serve at once.

CHICKEN WITH GREEN OLIVES

Olives are a popular flavouring for poultry and game in Apulia in Italy, where this recipe originates. In Italy every bit of the bird is used in some way, most often for soups and stock.

SERVES 4

INGREDIENTS:
4 chicken breasts, part boned
2 tbsp olive oil
30 g/1 oz/2 tbsp butter
1 large onion, chopped finely
2 garlic cloves, crushed
2 red, yellow or green (bell) peppers,
    deseeded and cut into large pieces
250 g/8 oz large closed-cup
    mushrooms, sliced or quartered
175 g/6 oz tomatoes, peeled and
    halved
150 ml/¼ pint/⅔ cup dry white wine
125–175 g/4–6 oz/⅔–1 cup green
    olives, pitted
4–6 tbsp double (heavy) cream
salt and pepper
chopped flat-leafed parsley, to garnish
pasta or tiny new potatoes, to serve

1 Season the chicken with salt and pepper. Heat the oil and butter in a frying pan (skillet), add the chicken and fry until browned all over. Remove from the pan and keep warm.

2 ▼ Add the onion and garlic to the pan and fry gently until beginning to soften. Add the (bell) peppers and the mushrooms and continue to cook for a few minutes longer.

3 ▲ Add the tomatoes and plenty of seasoning to the pan, and then transfer the vegetable mixture to an ovenproof casserole. Place the chicken on the bed of vegetables.

4 Add the wine to the pan and bring to the boil. Pour the wine over the chicken and cover the casserole. Cook in a preheated oven, 180°C/350°F/ Gas Mark 4, for 50 minutes.

5 ▼ Add the olives to the chicken, mix lightly then pour on the cream. Cover the casserole and return to the oven for 10–20 minutes or until the chicken is very tender.

6 Adjust the seasoning and serve the pieces of chicken, surrounded by the vegetables and sauce, with pasta or tiny new potatoes. Sprinkle with parsley to garnish.

ROMAN CHICKEN

This Roman dish is equally good cold and could be taken on a picnic – serve with bread to mop up the juices.

SERVES 4

INGREDIENTS:

4 tbsp olive oil
6 chicken pieces
4 large mixed red, green and yellow (bell) peppers
1 large red onion, sliced
2 garlic cloves, crushed with 1 tsp salt
125 g/4 oz/⅔ cup pitted green olives
Tomato Sauce (page 43)
300 ml/½ pint/1¼ cups hot chicken stock
2 sprigs fresh marjoram
salt and pepper

1 ▼ Heat half the oil in a flameproof casserole and brown the chicken pieces on all sides. Remove the chicken pieces and set aside.

2 ▼ Remove the seeds and the cores from the (bell) pepper and cut them into strips.

3 ▲ Add the remaining oil to the casserole. Fry the onion gently for 5–7 minutes until just softened, then add the garlic and fry for another minute. Stir in the (bell) peppers, olives and tomato sauce and bring to the boil.

4 ▼ Return the chicken to the casserole and add the stock and the marjoram. Cover the casserole and simmer gently for about 45 minutes until the chicken is tender. Season to taste with salt and pepper, and serve with warm crusty bread.

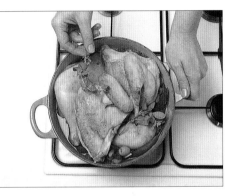

COQ AU VIN BLANC

Small pieces of chicken are gently simmered with wine, herbs, bacon, mushrooms and onions to produce a dish reminiscent of an authentic French meal.

SERVES 2

INGREDIENTS:
2 chicken leg quarters
4 thick lean back bacon slices, derinded
2 tbsp oil
125 g/4 oz button onions or 1 large onion, sliced
1 garlic clove, crushed
150 ml/¹⁄₄ pint/²⁄₃ cup dry white wine
300 ml/¹⁄₂ pint/1¹⁄₄ cups chicken stock
1 bay leaf
large pinch of dried oregano
1 tbsp cornflour (cornstarch)
60 g/2 oz/³⁄₄ cup tiny button mushrooms, trimmed
salt and pepper
chopped fresh parsley, to garnish
boiled rice or creamed potatoes, to serve

1 ▼ Cut each chicken leg into two pieces and season well with salt and pepper. Cut the bacon slices into 1 cm/½ inch strips.

2 Heat the oil in a large saucepan. Fry the chicken until golden brown and remove from the pan. Add the bacon, onions and garlic, and fry until lightly browned. Drain off all the fat from the saucepan.

3 ▼ Add the wine, stock, bay leaf, oregano, and salt and pepper to the saucepan, then add the chicken to the pan and bring to the boil.

4 Cover the saucepan tightly and reduce the heat. Simmer very gently for 40–50 minutes, or until the chicken is very tender.

5 ▲ Blend the cornflour (cornstarch) with a little cold water and add to the saucepan with the mushrooms. Bring back to the boil and simmer for a further 5 minutes.

6 Adjust the seasoning, discard the bay leaf. Serve sprinkled liberally with chopped parsley, and with boiled rice or creamed potatoes.

COUNTRY CHICKEN CASSEROLE

Most ceramic casserole dishes can be used with care on the hob, but something called a diffuser should be placed between the heat and the dish – it is usually a double layer of perforated metal holding the dish off the heat. However, if you are unsure, simply sauté the chicken and transfer to an ovenproof serving dish.

SERVES 4

INGREDIENTS:
1 free-range chicken, 1.5 kg/ 3 lb, cut into 6–8 pieces
flour for dusting
30 g/1 oz/2 tbsp butter
1 tsp olive oil
10 pickling onions
3 garlic cloves, unpeeled
1 carrot, diced
1 celery stalk, diced
1 bay leaf
125 g/4 oz smoked streaky bacon, diced
600 ml/1 pint/2½ cups stock, or to cover
750 g/1½ lb waxy potatoes, sliced
salt and pepper

1 ▲ Rinse and pat dry the chicken pieces. Dust with flour. Melt the butter with the oil over medium-high heat and brown the chicken pieces well all over, then set aside.

2 ▲ Add the onions, garlic, carrot, celery, bay leaf and bacon to the pan. Cook over a medium heat for 10 minutes, and season well. Return the chicken to the pan and pour over the stock. Check the seasoning.

3 ▼ Arrange the sliced potatoes over the top of the casserole. Cover and simmer for 1 hour.

4 Serve piping hot with a green vegetable.

CHICKEN WITH RICE & PEAS

This dish, which is also known as chicken pelau, is a national favourite in Trinidad and Tobago. The secret of a good pelau is that it must be brown in colour, which is achieved by caramelizing the chicken first.

SERVES 6

INGREDIENTS:
1 onion, chopped
2 garlic cloves
1 tbsp chopped fresh chives
1 tbsp chopped fresh thyme
2 celery stalks with leaves, chopped
350 ml/12 fl oz/1½ cups water
½ fresh coconut, chopped
liquid from 1 fresh coconut
500 g/16 oz can of pigeon peas or
*   kidney beans, drained*
1 red chilli, deseeded and sliced thinly
2 tbsp groundnut oil
2 tbsp caster (superfine) sugar
1.5 kg/3 lb chicken pieces
250 g/8 oz/1¼ cups white long-grain
*   rice, rinsed and drained*
salt and pepper
celery leaves, to garnish

1 Put the onion, garlic, chives, thyme, celery and 4 tablespoons of the water into a food processor and blend until smooth. Alternatively, chop the onion and celery very finely, then grind with the garlic and herbs in a pestle and mortar, gradually mixing in the water. Pour into a saucepan and set aside.

2 ▲ Put the chopped coconut and liquid into the food processor and mix to a thick milk, adding water if necessary. Alternatively, finely grate the coconut and mix with the liquid. Add to the onion and celery mixture.

3 Stir in the drained pigeon peas or kidney beans and chilli. Cook over a low heat for 15 minutes. Season to taste with salt and pepper.

4 ▲ Put the oil and sugar in a heavy-based casserole and cook over a moderate heat until the sugar begins to caramelize.

5 Add the chicken and cook for 15–20 minutes, turning frequently, until browned all over.

6 ▲ Stir in the coconut mixture, the rice and remaining water. Bring to the boil, then reduce the heat, cover and simmer for 20 minutes until the chicken and rice are tender and the liquid has been absorbed. Garnish with celery leaves and serve.

CHICKEN & VEGETABLE RICE

Boneless chicken breasts may be used instead of the drumsticks, in which case slash them diagonally.

SERVES 4–6

INGREDIENTS:

4 chicken drumsticks
3 tbsp mango chutney
1¹/₂ tbsp lemon juice
6 tbsp vegetable oil
1-2 tbsp medium or hot curry paste
1¹/₂ tsp paprika
1 large onion, chopped
125 g/4 oz button mushrooms
2 carrots, sliced thinly
2 celery sticks, trimmed and sliced thinly
¹/₂ aubergine (eggplant), quartered and sliced
2 garlic cloves, crushed
¹/₂ tsp ground cinnamon
250 g/8 oz/1¹/₄ cups long-grain rice
600 ml/1 pint/2¹/₂ cups chicken stock or water
60 g/2 oz frozen peas or sliced French (green) beans
60 g/2 oz/¹/₃ cup seedless raisins
salt and pepper

TO GARNISH:

hard-boiled (hard-cooked) egg slices
lemon slices (optional)

1 ▼ Slash the drumsticks twice on each side, cutting through the skin and deep into the flesh. Mix the chutney with the lemon juice, 1 tablespoon of the oil, the curry paste and paprika. Brush over the drumsticks and reserve the remainder for later.

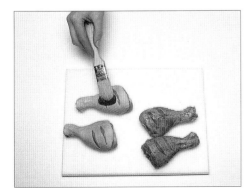

2 Heat 2 tablespoons of oil in the frying pan (skillet) and fry the drumsticks for about 5 minutes until sealed and golden brown all over.

3 ▲ Meanwhile, heat the remaining oil in a saucepan, add the onion, mushrooms, carrots, celery, aubergine (eggplant), garlic and cinnamon, and fry for 1 minute. Stir in the rice and cook for 1 minute, stirring until the rice is coated with the oil. Add the stock and the remaining mango chutney mixture, peas, raisins, and seasoning. Mix and bring to the boil.

4 ▼ Reduce the heat and add the drumsticks to the mixture, pushing them down into the liquid. Cover and cook gently for 25 minutes until the liquid is absorbed, the drumsticks are tender and the rice is cooked.

5 Remove the drumsticks from the pan and keep warm. Fluff up the rice mixture and transfer to a warm serving plate. Arrange the rice in a nicely shaped mound and place the drumsticks around it. Garnish the dish with wedges of hard-boiled (hard-cooked) egg and lemon slices, if using.

JAMBALAYA

Jambalaya, New Orlean's paella, dates back to the 18th century, when it was served as slave food. Today, this hearty rice dish can contain any number of meats, such as chicken, duck, ham or sausage.

SERVES 4

INGREDIENTS:

60 g/2 oz/4 tbsp butter
2 onions, chopped
2 garlic cloves, crushed
5 celery stalks, chopped
1 red (bell) pepper, deseeded and
    chopped
1 green (bell) pepper, deseeded and
    chopped
1 tsp Cajun Spice Mixture (page 74)
250 g/8 oz/1¼ cups long-grain rice
425 g/14 oz can of tomatoes, drained
    and chopped
500 g/1 lb cooked assorted meats
    (chicken, duck, ham or sausage),
    sliced or diced
250 ml/8 fl oz/1 cup vegetable stock or
    white wine
1 tsp salt
parsley sprigs, to garnish

1 Melt the butter in a large, heavy-based pan. Add the onions, garlic, celery, (bell) peppers and Cajun spice mixture and mix well.

2 ▲ Add the rice and stir well to coat the grains in the butter mixture.

3 ▼ Add the tomatoes, meats, stock or wine and salt. Bring to the boil, stirring well.

4 Reduce the heat, cover and simmer for about 15 minutes or until the rice is cooked and fluffy and has absorbed all the liquid. If the mixture seems to be too dry then add a little boiling water, tablespoon by tablespoon, towards the end of the cooking time.

5 Serve the jamabalaya on warm plates, garnished with parsley.

BATON ROUGE CHICKEN GUMBO

Everyone in the state of Louisiana, USA, has their own favourite gumbo recipe. This one uses chicken with prawns (shrimp), okra and a little belly of pork: a recipe that is hard to improve upon.

SERVES 4–6

INGREDIENTS:
30 g/1 oz/2 tbsp butter
1 tbsp corn oil
30 g/1 oz/1/4 cup plain (all-purpose) flour
90 g/3 oz belly of pork, sliced
1 large onion, sliced
2 celery stalks, chopped
500 g/1 lb okra, trimmed and sliced
425 g/14 oz can of peeled tomatoes
2 garlic cloves, crushed
1 litre/1³/4 pints/4 cups chicken stock
   or water
250 g/8 oz peeled prawns (shrimp)
500 g/1 lb skinless cooked chicken, cut
   into bite-sized pieces
1 tsp Tabasco sauce
500 g/1 lb/3 cups hot cooked rice, to
   serve

1 ▼ Heat the butter and oil in a small, heavy-based pan. Add the flour and cook, stirring frequently, over a low heat until the roux turns a rich brown colour. Set aside.

2 Meanwhile, in a large pan, fry the pork slices gently, without extra fat, until they are golden brown on all sides and the fat has been rendered. Add the sliced onion and celery, and cook for a further 5 minutes.

3 ▼ Stir in the okra and fry gently for a further 3 minutes. Stir in the tomatoes and garlic, and simmer over gentle heat for 15 minutes.

4 Gradually add the stock to the browned roux, mixing and blending well, then add to the okra mixture. Cover and simmer for 1 hour.

5 ▲ Add the prawns (shrimp) and chicken to the okra mixture, cook for a further 5 minutes until the chicken is thoroughly reheated. Stir in the Tabasco sauce.

6 Spoon the gumbo into individual serving bowls and top with a scoop of hot cooked rice.

CHICKEN ETOUFFE

Etouffé means smothered and is a popular way of presenting food in Cajun cuisine. Here, strips of chicken and vegetables are smothered in a thickened dark sauce flavoured with basil.

SERVES 4–6

INGREDIENTS:

60 g/2 oz/4 tbsp butter
1 small onion, chopped
1 celery stalk, chopped
1 small green (bell) pepper, deseeded and chopped
1 red (bell) pepper, deseeded and chopped
1 small red chilli, deseeded and finely chopped
1 tsp Cajun Spice Mixture (page 74)
1 tsp chopped fresh basil
2 tbsp vegetable oil
2 tbsp flour
500 ml/16 fl oz/2 cups rich chicken stock
500 g/1 lb skinless, boneless chicken breasts, cut into strips or bite-sized pieces
4 spring onions (scallions), chopped
salt
rice or couscous, to serve

1 ▼ Melt the butter in a large, heavy-based pan. Add the onion, celery, green and red (bell) peppers and chilli and cook over a gentle heat until softened, about 5 minutes.

2 Add the Cajun spice mixture, basil and salt. Cook for a further 2 minutes.

3 Meanwhile, heat the oil in a pan, add the flour and cook, slowly, until a rich reddish-brown roux is formed. Whisk constantly to prevent the roux from scorching and becoming bitter.

4 ▼ Gradually add the stock and whisk well to make a smooth thickened sauce. Pour the sauce over the vegetable mixture and allow to simmer for about 15 minutes.

5 ▼ Add the chicken strips and the spring onions (scallions) and cook for a further 10 minutes, stirring occasionally until the chicken is cooked and tender.

6 Serve with cooked long-grain rice or freshly cooked fluffy couscous.

GRILLADES WITH GRITS

Grillades is a Cajun meat and vegetable stew in a thick gravy. It is considered to be Bayou breakfast food and would always be served with grits, a kind of creamy cereal (not unlike porridge) made from corn.

SERVES 6

INGREDIENTS:

4 tbsp olive oil
1 kg/2 lb skinless, boneless chicken breasts, cut into 7 × 10 cm/3 × 4 inch strips
60 g/2 oz/½ cup plain (all-purpose) flour
3 onions, chopped
2 green (bell) peppers, deseeded and chopped
4 celery stalks, chopped finely
1 garlic clove, crushed
500 g/1 lb ripe tomatoes, peeled, deseeded and chopped
2 tbsp tomato purée (paste)
1 tsp chopped fresh thyme
½–1 tsp Tabasco sauce
1½ tsp paprika
¼ tsp cayenne pepper
1 tsp salt
150 ml/¼ pint/⅔ cup vegetable stock
150 ml/¼ pint/⅔ cup white wine
hominy grits or couscous, to serve

1 ▼ Heat the oil in a heavy-based frying pan (skillet). Add the chicken strips and fry quickly on both sides until no longer pink. Remove with a perforated spoon and set aside.

2 ▼ Add the flour to the pan juices and mix well, until the flour is absorbed by the juices. Cook over a moderate heat, stirring constantly, until the roux changes to a rich brown colour.

3 Add the onions, (bell) peppers, celery and garlic, and mix well. Cover and cook over a gentle heat for about 15 minutes until softened.

4 ▲ Return the chicken to the pan with the tomatoes, tomato purée (paste), thyme, Tabasco sauce, paprika, cayenne, salt, stock and wine, mixing well.

5 Cover and simmer gently for a further 40–45 minutes, or until the chicken and vegetables are cooked. Serve hot with hominy grits, if liked, or couscous.

INDEX